TANGLED IN TURQUOISE

Bobbi Davari

TANGLED IN TURQUOISE

First published in the United States, 2015

A catalogue record for this book is available from the British Library

ISBN 9781517088149

Printed and bound in the United States

Bobbi Davari

This, too, shall pass

TANGLED IN TURQUOISE

AUTHOR'S NOTE

I have changed the names of some of the people in this book for their protection.

TANGLED IN TURQUOISE

CONTENTS

ACKNOWLEDGMENTS

My thanks go, particularly, to Marj and Dave for their unwavering support over the past fifty years, and to all those people—too numerous to mention—who helped me find 'The Way', even when the path seemed quite misty.

Special thanks, also, to Liz Reed for reading and re-reading this manuscript with such eagerness and excitement, that, after her enthusiastic encouragement, I couldn't do anything other than publish it!

TANGLED IN TURQUOISE

CHAPTER ONE

INCHING ALONG IN THE FAST LANE

The traffic was at a standstill with a long tail-back from the traffic lights. They were barely visible from where we sat. The midday temperature—around 35°C—was becoming unbearable, even with air-conditioning in the car. Trying to remain still in this heat was difficult. Sweat trickled down my forehead and under the rim of my sunglasses as we sat in silence, watching the distant lights change to green, at which, each car inched its way forward a yard or two. Tehran's traffic problems are famous throughout Iran, and those who've lived here and have left the country, still recall stories of things that have happened as they waited in those long lines of traffic.

The driver pushed back his cap and glanced in the rear-view mirror whilst mopping his brow. He pulled the black peak over his forehead again and repositioned his cap.

Suddenly, a young teenage boy appeared from nowhere and threw a soapy sponge onto the windscreen. He yanked back the wipers and began vigorously washing the window. Asdollah, the driver, motioned to him to stop.

Nakon, pesar, machine kasif mishé. (Stop it sonny, you'll make the car dirty.)

But, determined to earn his *pangzar* (five rials) the boy continued, refusing to listen. He began singing a funny pop song which made us laugh, and he finally won us over. Asdollah handed him the money, more for the boy's entertainment and plucky persistence than anything else. The boy then moved on to the car in front to repeat his performance. We giggled as we watched him.

The lights changed to green, we crept forward a little but quickly came to a standstill again. The routine was so familiar. Every Thursday, without fail, we would travel along this route to meet up with my husband, Hamid, at his parents' house for lunch. Sometimes, other relatives or family friends were there when we arrived. Most were cheerful, friendly people who loved nothing better than eating good food, telling jokes and gossiping!

Sanil Moulouk, my mother-in-law, was an excellent cook and praised by many for her generous hospitality. She was the daughter of a wealthy tea merchant in Tehran, and an only child, until her mother died of tuberculosis in her early thirties, and her father re-married. He had two children by his second wife, by which time Sanil Moulouk had married Hamid's father, who was then a young cavalry officer in Reza Shah's army.

My father-in-law, Abdol Hussein, was now a General in Mohammad Reza Shah's army and also the Shah's Special Aide, by

Sanil Moulouk, my mother-in-law

Abdol Hussein, my father-in-law

the time I arrived in Tehran. He served his country for over forty years in the army, and after he retired, became head of the armed forces medical insurance until the Iranian revolution took place in 1979.

He was a quiet, kindly man, a devout Moslem, with simple tastes. His life at home was strictly routine, which at times, irritated his wife. But despite her complaints, he still continued to live this way.

He came from a military family and, according to my husband, Abdol Hussein's father went off to fight a Turkish war when my father-in-law was a small boy. He was away from home seven years, and during that time, never contacted his wife. She, after a certain time, assumed he had been killed in action, so married again. At the end of seven years he returned home only to find that he had been replaced by Agha Sepir, who then became my father-in-law's step-father.

Agha Sepir was an historian who later became Minister of Education. When he eventually died, his wife married again, showing clearly that she was a women who firmly believed in marriage!

Privileges were many for us at that time, doors that were firmly shut to others opened without a squeak for us. We lived at the top level of society and enjoyed a comfortable life. Later, I gradually realized how much this blinded me to the plight and needs of others as I accepted the division between social classes -

that was until the day we were stuck in Tehran's traffic, where my story began.

RESIGNATION CREPT IN AS WE WAITED.

Khaili shulloogeh, (It's very crowded) complained Asdolla as people weaved in and out among the still-standing traffic. Another young boy, his hair black and unkempt, appeared at the window with a small tray of assorted items: easy-wipe chamois leathers, dangling furry dice, sweets and chocolate bars.

Agha, panjeraiat khaeli kasseefe, yedoone as in chamois bekhar. (Sir, your windows are really dirty, buy one of these chamois.)

His smile and, again, the persistent sales patter we'd experienced with our young 'window cleaner' only a few minutes before, warmed us to him as we realized that he, too, was determined to sell us something. Such spirit in one so young is hard to resist, but charming and persuasive though he was, we declined his offers. He moved away, fixing his gaze on the car in front.

There were many of these boys in Tehran from poor families, learning how to make a living from a very early age.

WE'D BEEN STUCK IN THIS LINE of traffic for almost half an hour now, and I was getting irritable as the noon-day heat intensified. I tried distracting myself from the situation by focusing on other things. At the same time, a soldier walked by and, spotting the car's number plate, saluted, something I was getting used to. It reminded me of the time when soldiers on guard duty outside government buildings presented arms as the car drove past. I was becoming aware of the level of 'difference' because of the family's status and beginning to enjoy the feelings of 'importance' connected with my in-laws.

My musings were interrupted by a tap on the window. I looked round but didn't see anyone, so turned and looked ahead at the traffic in front. Another tap, I turned and looked again, expecting to see someone at the window and saw no-one, but was aware something had happened. Another tap, this time I swung my head round hoping to catch sight of who was trying to get my attention. As I did, I saw a hand drop down from the window. I shuffled over to the door, wound down the window and poked my head outside.

Kharnoum, yeh toman beddeh man (Lady, give me one toman (10 rials)).

The voice came up from the pavement. I looked down and was shocked to see a man sitting on a trolley made from an old pram. He had no legs, and the rest of his body was quite small, but, despite his condition, he seemed fit and cheerful. He wore a white shirt with sleeves rolled up to his elbows, and his black trouser legs were tucked under him. I rummaged inside my bag trying to find my purse then handed him a few coins, for which he seemed grateful.

My eyes followed him as he pushed his trolley away from

the car using his hands flat against the hot, dirty pavement. As I wound up the window I had an overwhelming sense of his physical disability and poverty, and of my own contrasting situation. There, but for the grace of God, go I, is quite a sobering thought. I genuinely felt ashamed as I acknowledged the influence my newly privileged life was having in causing me to feel socially superior, attitudes that contrasted with my newly found Christian faith. But I now see that God was already working in me, teaching me lessons about His love for *all people,* regardless of their status, and that this was only the beginning.

CHAPTER TWO

HUMBLE BEGINNINGS

I was born in Britain just after the Second World War in 1947, one of six children, all girls, and next to youngest. My father was an engineer's draughtsman in a government organisation by day, and a part-time maths and technical drawing lecturer at a local college in the evenings. He was a gifted man who loved music, but had little time to exercise and develop his interests. I still remember those late nights as a young teenager, lying in bed listening to him repeating phrases of Chopin's *Nocturnes* on the piano, or picking his way through various exercises on the guitar in the stillness of the house when everyone had gone to bed. He was a quiet, intellectual man, who distanced himself from his children. Looking back, I can now see that he saw his role as provider for his family, and that my mother's role was to look after the children.

Money was always short—1947 was not the best time, financially, to be born—and this affected the way we lived. We were quite poor by today's standards and this brought with it many restrictions and pressures in those early years.

Dad, when I was a child

Mum and dad, Jenny and me (to the left)

My mother did her very best to keep us all fed and clothed on the small amount of housekeeping she received from my father. She was a good cook and an exceptional baker, whose strawberry flans, fruit pies, scones and bread were the best I've ever tasted. The delicious smell of fruit stewing still takes me back to the kitchen of our family home. At mealtimes, because there were so many of us, everything laid out before us was usually eaten up with no leftovers - and often we argued about who'd eaten what. So mealtimes were usually spent eating and squabbling, being told off and threatened with punishment, but mostly being sent to our rooms. I hated being sent to my room, but never seemed to catch on to the fact that this was likely to happen if I misbehaved. I was still very young and hopeful that things might change.

Once, when I was about eight years old, I was sent to my room, and, as usual, hated being forcibly confined. I was quite upset and remember looking out of the bedroom window only to see the neighbours' children freely playing in their back gardens. I suddenly had the idea that if I climbed out of the window onto the roof I could escape and no-one would be any the wiser. So, determined but fearful, I climbed out of the window backwards, onto the gently sloped roof that curved up at the end (later providing a handy foothold) and, still hanging on to the window frame, legs dangling and chest flat against the slates, I looked down to find out how far away the guttering was so that I could slide down, grab hold of it and leap to freedom. I was struggling to make my short legs stretch that far down when all of a sudden I heard:

What **do** *you think you're doing? Come down here at once!* (My mother's 'dulcet' tone!)

I'm stuck, I replied, *I can't get down.*

Try pulling yourself up and climb back through the window, she yelled.

But I couldn't. My arms, which had been bearing my entire body weight for quite some time were too weak now.

I can't do it. I whimpered, knowing that big trouble lay ahead.

Mum was now in control of my escape! I turned my head to look down at her and saw crowds of people looking up at me—the neighbours, (my betrayers!). Then, the same glowering figure I had just seen beneath me, was suddenly above me at the window. She reached down, took hold of my arms and hauled me back into my bedroom. This was followed by a very loud telling off and a good smack. Her last words as she left the room were:

Don't ever do that again! And I didn't, ever...but there were other things…

MUM WAS ALSO AN EXCELLENT DRESSMAKER AND KNITTER. She made her own and all her girls' coats, dresses, skirts, shorts, swimsuits, cardigans, Aran sweaters, hats and mittens, and was very fussy about us being 'well turned out' because she seemed quite concerned about what the neighbours might think of us.

She was always busy with her chores which took precedence over spending time relating to or relaxing with the children, and she tended to issue commands, often followed by threats when she became impatient. We were always being told what to do and what not to do, and our personal choice in a matter never entered her mind, I'm sure. Consequently, there were many upsets as wills clashed and often these clashes ended up with some kind of punishment. I was carefree in those early years, it seems now, but there was always an 'undercurrent' of hostility towards me from my mother.

MY WEEKLY ROUTINE DURING the school term was pretty much the same. I'd go to school in the morning, come home in the afternoon, do my homework and then go out and play with the neighbours' children. When the light evenings and good weather arrived, I found it difficult to stay in the house because it was small and crowded and full of bossy people. On Saturdays, a gang of us young children would meet up and decide what to do for the day.

There was a park directly opposite our house which was usually the first place we'd head for to play football or cricket, because our gang consisted mostly of boys. I was hopeless at both but did my best! Other times, when the weather was warmer, we would trail through nearby woods looking for birds' nests and hazelnuts, or trek up to Strelley Village to take turns sliding down the sandbanks, only to receive a scolding from mum for being completely covered in red dust when I arrived back home.

Playing marbles was a favourite activity and fierce competition between the children led to high levels of skilful games. This was something I was good at and took very seriously.

During a game one Saturday afternoon as we all crouched over the marbles, intent on beating our opponents, a group of young boys going home from the 'threp'ny rush' at the cinema down the road, started bothering us. This started a fight between them and our boys, who eventually 'saw the lads off'. But as we resumed the game, one of the lads gave a shout, and a large stone hit the back of my little sister's head. She was very young, about four years old, and screaming now at the top of her lungs. Terrified by the sight of blood pouring out of her head and worried that she might suffer brain damage, we started panicking. The game was immediately abandoned and our lads chased after the antagonists, while the girls spent the rest of the afternoon trying to console my frightened little sister, and mopping up the blood through her ginger curls. Needless to say, I was in trouble again when my mother, who was horrified at the sight of all that blood, scolded me severely for not taking care of Jenny properly.

On Sundays we were sent to Sunday school—a small wooden hut run by Brethren Christians—but more to give my mother a break than any spiritual concerns my parents had.

ONE OF MY GREATEST PLEASURES AS A CHILD was singing, and

while Bill Haley rocked the world with *Rock Around the Clock*, I was accepted in to the Player Junior School Choir just after my eighth birthday. The choir consisted of two groups of girls. One group sang soprano parts and the other, alto. I was an alto.

Miss Wenn, our smiling, bespectacled choir mistress, made each choir practise a joy to be involved in, away from the plod of academic study. She was musically gifted as both a pianist and singer, and made vinyl recordings of her rich, alto voice singing classical works and spiritual songs from the black community. She was also gifted in the intelligent way she was able to maintain a gentle control over a large bunch of giggling, young children as they sang the wrong bits when attempting new songs. This she did by laughing with us and then moved swiftly on to the next thing, gaining our attention again.

I think what she did with us was quite ambitious, teaching us the music of a song by first playing it through on the piano, then listening as we tried to sing it back to her to see if we had grasped it—both parts, soprano and alto—then repeated this process until she was 'happy' with the result. I can't remember ever being given any sheets of music with the songs, only the words. Using this method she was able to teach us the music to songs like *The Bird Catcher's Song* from Mozart's *Magic Flute; All in the April Evening;* sea shanties, spirituals, and many others. These we sang not only for our own school's concerts, but at other schools, too. We also competed with other choirs within the Nottingham area, and once, after a performance, I was handed a huge chocolate Easter egg, wrapped in pale green, shiny paper and filled with chocolates, as a reward.

These were happy times of fun, laughter and music (what more could a child want) and since then, music has been one of my best loved and closest companions in life. Through both happy and sad times, music has brought joy and comfort to me in a way that no person has ever been able to. Those notes, chords and phrases, special only to me, reaching deep inside my spirit, soothing the hurts of times past, and promising a future of never being alone: the composer understood exactly how to reach me.

My family wasn't as thrilled with my spontaneous musical outbursts as much as Miss Wenn was, and I was continually being told to 'pipe down' as I went round the house singing. But I found it so difficult to do because the 'song' was in my heart.

AT HOME, FINDING SPACE TO DAY-DREAM and develop as an individual was quite impossible. Living in a small house full of people who were always talking or arguing, poking fun at and annoying each other, demanded my attention. Being the next to youngest made me vulnerable to my older sisters who enjoyed teasing me by laughing at me and ridiculing things I said. This often ended up in tears because, eventually, I would get upset at being continually provoked and would strike out at one of them, which was just what they wanted to start a squabble, and this was how we related to each other, mostly.

I was an energetic, restless and cheeky youngster who often felt my mother's restrictive attitude to my plans for the day unreasonable. So I would go and climb the lilac tree in the garden 'forgetting' that she had told me not to, or come home late from playing with the neighbouring children. This sort of disobedient behaviour increased, along with the scoldings and beatings, and, as time went on, I began to feel like an outsider in my own family and was often puzzled by my mother's hostility to me. She would say: *I never wanted you,* which, in time, took hold of my mind every time I heard it.

One day, when I was a young teenager, she became more violent than I had ever seen before. She was always very quick and I was always taken by surprise. She started shouting at me for something and as I tried to respond, she started hitting me and didn't stop. It was as if she was venting her own frustrations in life on me. Blow after blow the fists came down in rapid succession, as did her angry threats. Then suddenly she stopped, briskly turned and, issuing commands as she went, left the room. I lay hurting and sobbing in my bedroom, feeling unloved and unwanted. I lay there all night but no-one came to see if I was all right. No-one came offering compassion or a warm drink or a comforting word. And that night in the lonely darkness, the thought crept into my mind that she really *didn't* want me, that she really *did hate me.* This broke my spirit and affected my life from then on.

I made several attempts to win back her favour, but these

were futile. Her coldness towards me, along with my father's indifference, made me start thinking that I wasn't their child at all and that they must have adopted me. The torment this thought had over me was overwhelmingly powerful, and I waited for the day when no-one else was at home so that I could search through the drawers to find my adoption papers and confirm my suspicions. Of course, when that day arrived, I couldn't find any papers because there weren't any, and this puzzled me even more as I tried to understand how my mother—as my real mother—could be so cold and so cruel to her own child. I became a sullen, unhappy person as a result, and felt displaced in my family.

My school work and my grades suffered dramatically. My form teacher took me aside one day and asked if anything was troubling me, but I was so frightened to discuss the situation at home that I told her there was nothing wrong. She challenged me about my falling grades, but, not really understanding why my work had deteriorated, I didn't say anything. I was sent to the deputy head who also wanted to know if anything was wrong. She advised me to follow my older sister 'who was a good example', which didn't help because we were always squabbling at home. I left her office with a sense of having failed both in my school work and everyone's eyes.

Next, and without any warning, came the educational psychologist, although I didn't know that at the time. He was kind and gentle as he asked if I could identify anything in the strange pictures he placed in front of me. Afterwards, he said I could go back to my classroom, and I left thinking that the session had been a bit odd.

Nothing more was said about it again and that seemed to be the end of the matter, as far as I was aware. I never found out whether or not the school had contacted my parents to see if they knew anything about the change in my behaviour, and life at school resumed the same as it had been before all this.

In the meantime, I had begun seeking the companionship lacking at home in the company of friends whose parents were kind to me.

I left Peveril Bilateral School in 1962, unqualified, and two months after my fifteenth birthday. I had no idea about the type of work I wanted to do, so took up a post as an office junior at a local stationery company, but left there within a year to do more or less the same kind of work at a firm of accountants.

At seventeen, I talked my way onto a secretarial course at a local college, with the hope that the skills learned on the course would enable me to get a better job. But when I got home and told my mother I had been accepted on the course, she was furious and completely against it, adding that they (my parents) would not support me. I was so shocked and deeply hurt by her reaction and felt even more rejected by her lack of encouragement about the course positively benefiting my future. Despite her objections I went ahead with it, and got a 'Saturday' job, but both my heart and mind were troubled knowing that I was going directly against my mother's wishes.

My mother's attitude towards me had become almost an obsession by now and a lot of my time was spent wondering why she was so horrible to me, and why she didn't want me to progress in life. Any good idea I had that seemed 'good' to me, was promptly squashed. Years later I figured out it must have been because, when I stopped work and went to college, I stopped bringing home my salary. This I gave to her (although it didn't amount to much in those days) and she gave me pocket-money. I later discovered that she was able to get some compensation while I was at college through her family allowance and other concessions, but she never let on, and the guilt hung heavy each time she reminded me that *they were keeping me.*

But little did I know how much going to college that year would change the course of my life…

CHAPTER THREE

TENDER TRAPPINGS

The first time I noticed Hamid was in the college common room one coffee break. He was leaning with his back to the wall over the other side of the room, laughing with a group of students. He was handsome and appeared confident as he chatted and repeatedly had his listeners in fits of laughter. I watched him the whole time and noticed there was a certain arrogance about him which, perversely, seemed enticing. I made up my mind there and then to invite him to a party I was going to at the weekend.

Moving over to his group, I began talking to Jack, another friend, and gradually included Hamid in our conversation. I then invited them both to the party, and we arranged to meet up in the city centre near the lions' statues in front of the Council House, known to the locals as the Market Square.

Jack was first to arrive, then me. Hamid was quite late and later told me that this was a sign of a person's importance in Iran. As we waited, Jack and I began dancing an exaggerated waltz in front of the Council House steps to music floating through the square. I stopped dancing as I caught sight of a slim, stunning figure walking towards us, immaculately dressed in a dark suit and snazzy tie (it *was* the sixties). I couldn't quite believe it was him; he looked *so* gorgeous!

As he greeted us he smiled and revealed a row of perfectly even teeth, ultra-white against his light brown, clean-shaven face. His dark eyes twinkled when he laughed, and his short, dark, gelled hair caught the light as we made our way over to the party. I couldn't take my eyes off him - I was hooked!

Nothing you could say can tear me away from my guy
Nothing you could do cos I'm stuck like glue to my guy

welcomed us as the party's door opened to reveal smooching couples on the dance floor, too engrossed in each other to keep time with the music. And later that night as China tested its first atomic bomb far, far away, we began a very turbulent courtship that lasted for the next five and a half years.

WE WERE MARRIED THE WEEK BEFORE CHRISTMAS 1970 at the Registry Office in the city. I was fifteen minutes late—held up at the hairdresser's—and rushed through the door to a very nervous husband-to-be who promptly told me off for being late! I adjusted my long, pink dress, slipped off my silver shoe, and pulled the toe piece of my tights forward to cover the hole my big toe had made.

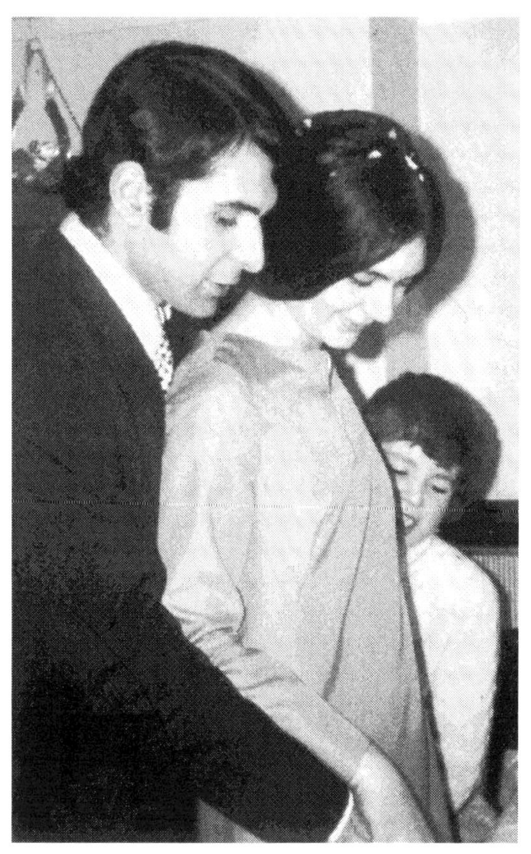

Cutting our wedding cake

We entered a room where family and friends were seated, stumbled over our promises, and left as husband and wife—for better, for worse, for richer or for poorer, in sickness and in health, for as long as we both shall live…

Three weeks later, Hamid was on a plane heading home to his family and his beloved Iran without me. His plan was to go back to Iran and do his national service for two years while I stayed in Britain. He thought I would be better off here in the UK with my family, rather than on my own with unfamiliar people and surroundings. But the thought of not seeing him for two years was more than I could bear. I loved him so much and didn't cope well with the separation. He tried to reason with me over the phone saying that I would be on my own a lot of the time if I went, but I didn't listen - all I wanted was to see him, to be with him.

So, after six months I decided to go to Iran. I didn't consult my family about it at all as, by this time, all relationships with them had broken down. But I remember my mother actually crying the morning I left home and just before I left, she handed me some money she had saved for me, saying she wished she could have given me more. I was stunned by this, and that she would even care about me leaving. I thought she would be glad to get rid of me at long last.

Before I left Britain Hamid advised me to apply for an Iranian passport at the Iranian Embassy in London. I travelled down to London by train, but, unfortunately, was late for my appointment. When I arrived, I was promptly escorted to a large, well furnished office, where, standing up as I entered the room, a man greeted me with:

Good morning, you are thirteen minutes late.

He then told me to sit down. I apologised and told him I had travelled down from Nottingham, but he refused to accept my explanation. I was quite upset by this. He asked for my documents, looked through them, told me to take them downstairs to a certain person who would process them, then return them to him. I left the room feeling slightly hurt and unjustly treated, not knowing this type of behaviour was quite normal in Iran. When I returned to his office I knocked on the door, which he opened and I handed him my documents. He continued talking to a man who was sitting in a comfortable chair in front of his desk. To my surprise he introduced me to his guest, who recognised my husband's family name. He told me that he had seen Hamid 'only last week at home', after visiting the family for lunch. Tears welled up in my eyes as he told me that Hamid was well and happy to be back in Iran. I wanted so much to see him. The other fellow handed me my papers wishing me a good journey and a happy life in Iran, adding that my husband was very fortunate to have such a beautiful wife! (Creep!)

Shortly after that, papers in order, I boarded the Iran Air plane to Tehran at Heathrow Airport on a brilliant, sunny, June morning, not knowing what I was going to or whether Hamid and I could be together when I got there. How blind love is…

CHAPTER FOUR

IN JUST SIX HOURS

The first thing to hit me was the heat as I stepped out of the plane onto the ramp at 2am the following morning. My cotton, short-sleeved, magenta outfit instantly warmed my body. In the distance I could see the bright lights of the 'Arrivals' section at Tehran Airport, where, eventually, my new Iranian passport was checked, but it took some time. I collected my luggage, thinking how small the building was compared to Heathrow Airport. I followed fellow passengers making their way out through an exit and into a large waiting room. A three foot high chrome rail separated new arrivals from the rest of the area and provided an aisle about ten feet wide, along which women with children, older parents and grandparents, and men, all back from visiting relatives in *Landan* (London) trundled along, tired and irritable from the long journey, pushing trolleys full of cases and Gucci and Harrods' carrier bags.

Bobbi, I'm over here.

I swung my head round in the direction of that familiar voice. There he was, smiling, tanned and *so* handsome, dressed in a white suit, holding a huge bouquet of white flowers. I could hardly contain the excitement I felt and just wanted to fling my arms round him, but the rail was between us and there were people in front of me still trying to make their way out. Finally out from the queue, I struggled with my cases towards Hamid. A soldier stepped forward, took hold of the luggage and placed it on the floor next to us. Then the much longed-for embrace I'd waited months for was cut short.

Not in public, he whispered in my ear.

He then introduced me to Asdollah, an army sergeant who was my father-in-law's official driver. Asdollah smilingly mumbled that he would put my cases in the car, and left us alone for a minute or two in the middle of the crowded airport.

Later, I came to learn that life was like that in Iran – full of people, and if you happened to be on your own for any reason, someone would come and sit with you and chat. They have a saying: *tanha naboshid* meaning, don't be alone. So if a person wanted to be alone—even husband and wife—it would be very difficult to achieve.

The oppressive heat made me feel uncomfortably self-conscious as we wandered out of the airport to the car where Asdollah was waiting for us. We sat in the back seat smiling and holding hands as we talked about my family back in Britain who, by now, seemed a million miles away. The airport lights faded in the background as the car steadily gathered speed along a dark road heading towards the city.

The first thing I spotted in the distance was a magnificent, illuminated tower.

That's the Shahyad Monument, recently built to commemorate 2,500 years of Iranian monarchy, said Hamid.

Getting nearer, I noticed that this huge construction had been built in the middle of a large island, whose immaculately turfed grounds were sectioned off by a honeycomb structure of pathways all the way around the base. Four wide, stone slabbed pathways with several uniform floodlit pools, each with its own gushing fountain, flanked either side of the pathways at quarterly intervals around the foot of the monument. The monument itself was beige coloured with a high, wide arch in the centre for people to walk through to the other side. The building stood on four separate, narrow legs that widened and pointed outward on the ground.

We drove on to Eisenhower Boulevard, then gradually joined Reza Shah Avenue where the streets and buildings were decorated with coloured lights and large images of Mohammad Reza Shah. The bright lights seemed to welcome us as we drove along and I felt happy and carefree.

We turned up Pahlavi Avenue - the longest avenue in Tehran - then into Abbasabad, where my parents-in-law then lived, and, after pulling up outside a large three-storey building, Asdollah got out of the car, rang the doorbell, then opened the car door for me. As he was taking my luggage from the car boot, the door of the house opened and a small, elderly-looking woman wearing a blue headscarf and a loose-fitting, *chadur* (a piece of cloth that normally covered a woman from head to foot, and could be worn in a number of ways) stood holding a square metal pan of something burning, producing a cloud of smoke in front of me as I walked over the threshold. This was Fatima, an old servant who had been with the family for many years. I walked towards Hamid's parents who greeted me warmly.

Welcome, they both said in unison. *How are you?*

I first met my mother-in-law in Germany, a trip we made to visit both her and Hamid's brother, who was doing his PhD there, before we were married. His father wasn't with them at that time, but I met him later on in Nottingham when he visited Hamid one summer.

Fine, thank you. I replied.

Threads of smoke rose from the kindled herb *Esfand* in the metal pan, a custom, I later learned, that is traditionally performed to ward off any evil spirits when someone new enters the home.

Salam, Khanoum, khushahmadi. (*Hello ma'am, welcome*) Fatima said repeatedly. Her bulbous, smiling face shone under the artificial light. I noticed how her tiny nose sat neatly between her large, rosy cheeks as she giggled. I smiled and walked along the hallway towards the stairs. A young man in his late teens, head shaved and wearing a khaki shirt and trousers, and brown, plastic flip flops, quickly took hold of my luggage and disappeared up the stairs, returning with the same alacrity to take the rest of the bags, all under my mother-in-law's instruction.

Chashm, kharnoum, (*Yes, ma'am*) he said, obediently.

His name was Ali and he was a young conscript who had been assigned to my father-in-law for domestic duties for the duration of his national service. I was then introduced to another man, Bahram, who stood alongside a young woman—his wife—holding a baby girl. Bahram had come to the house many years before also as a young conscript, and when the duration of his service ended - normally two years - asked if he could stay on and work for my father-in-law, which he did for many years until Baba died.

Befarmaid too. (*Come in*).

My mother-in-law beckoned us through the corridor into a large living room with huge Persian carpets covering every inch of the floor. The furniture was placed around the walls at either end of the room with small tables between chairs. The family's dining table sat in a recess opposite french windows that led out on to a veranda. She was talking to me all the time, but I didn't understand what she was saying.

She's asking if you'd like something to eat, said Hamid.

No thank you, I replied in English, *I had a meal on the plane, but I would like a glass of water, please.*

Hamid translated and the order for a glass of water was given to the boy, who scurried off into the kitchen, and returned with a glass of ice-cold water.

I sat down feeling tired but happy to finally be there with Hamid, and as they all chatted in Farsi, my eyes began taking in the room with its wall-to-wall Persian carpets. My mother-in-law kept speaking to me but I didn't understand what she said until Hamid translated. I was already beginning to feel a sense of 'them and me' because of the difficulty in trying to communicate, but then it was almost 4am by this time, so we agreed to continue our conversations over breakfast the following morning.

Our bedroom was on the second floor at the front of the house. It was a large room with a unit of several white wardrobes opposite a large bed with two large, pale and dark-blue persian rugs on either side. A white dressing table with a mirror and a matching chair stood against the side wall.

What's this? I said laughingly, picking up a white, flimsy negligee and robe, about four sizes too big, from the bed.

A mother-in-law's idea, was the reply, and with that, Hamid closed the door. We were alone together at last.

BRILLIANT SUNLIGHT SHONE THROUGH THE gap between the curtains as I woke the next morning. It seemed very early and already the temperature was quite warm. I heard my mother-in-law's wide awake, distant voice coming from downstairs. Hamid, already up and dressed, popped his head round the door:

We're waiting for you to come down and have breakfast.

He disappeared again and I lay in the quietness of our room. I focussed my gaze on the window as my mind started working. I'm here, I thought, here in Tehran with Hamid, and suddenly, I was fully awake!

Loud, high-pitched singing pierced the early morning quietness. I pulled back the curtain to see a street vendor leading a donkey over-loaded with fresh fruits, herbs and vegetables, in the street below. I later learned that these vendors sang their way round the streets of Tehran selling all manner of things to people, usually to housewives or their servants who, when they heard their special song (each merchant had his own) doors would swing open and women in chadurs and plastic flip-flops would come out to inspect their produce. The women would show their purses, then pick fault with the goods, haggle over the price and briskly walk away, flip-flops rhythmically slapping against their heels. The vendor would then call after them saying they couldn't find better quality anywhere else, to which they would either shriek an admonishing reply or return to haggle with him again.

Haggling is a part of life in Iran when shopping, and although you may not always win the tussle, traders expect you to haggle; if you don't, they lose their respect for you. Foreigners, not used to haggling, are often ripped off by traders.

Remembering Hamid and his parents were still waiting for me I quickly showered and dressed and descended the stairs feeling slightly apprehensive about what to expect.

Salem khanoum, sobh bekheir. (*Hello ma'am, good morning*)

Fatima greeted me enthusiastically. *Befarmaid too.*

She showed me into the room where the family was already having breakfast, after waiting quite a time for me to join them.

Good morning. My parents-in-law's cheery English welcome brought a smile to my face.

Good morning, I replied.

Fatimeh, chai bar sheir biar baraye Bobbi khanoum.

The order for tea with milk was given and my first breakfast in Iran began. After the initial politeness, the conversation became more focused between Hamid and his parents, so I sat quietly enjoying my breakfast of flat, crispy, buttered bread with honey dripping over the edges, soft boiled eggs, *panir* - like feta cheese, and tea with milk. (Iranians usually drink tea without milk.) A gentle, perfumed fragrance drew my attention to a saucer of small, white flower heads in the centre of the table. As the days went by, I noticed it was Baba's habit to walk in the garden in the cool of the early morning and pick a handful of *Maryam* flower-heads to place on the breakfast table.

Streaks of sunlight shone through the french windows as I sat next to Hamid, watching him, admiring him. He turned to me saying that he had to go to town for the morning but would be back for lunch.

But what will I do while you're gone? was my panicked response, afraid of being left alone with his parents and unable to communicate with them.

Oh, you'll be OK. Unpack your things and start settling in; I'll be back soon.

He said goodbye to his parents and left. I wandered back upstairs after several failed, but comical attempts to make myself understood. As I closed the door behind me I noticed several doors leading off from the square hallway and became aware that our bedroom was part of another apartment on the second floor of the house. Curiosity led me across the ceramic tiled floors where, on opening a door, I discovered a comfortably furnished sitting room with a large window. Next door to it was a very spacious, tiled kitchen where I would learn to cook Iranian food(!) Diagonally across from that was a large, elaborately furnished room with carved woodwork and a huge, lacquered dining-table, two large chandeliers hanging either end of the ceiling, and an expensive Russian clock sitting between two matching, ornate, period vases. Beautiful, dark blue Persian carpets with intricate floral patterns in contrasting colours covered the floor. I later discovered that this room was reserved for entertaining guests. We were permitted to use it, but not exclusively. But the rest of the apartment was ours to use and became 'home' for the next year.

Life in Tehran began to take on a pattern from my first day there. The routine of Hamid going off to work and of life with his parents had already been established by the time I arrived. Hamid seemed to think that I would slot into that easily without experiencing too much difficulty. And if I had just 'slotted in' it would have worked very well, but that wasn't the case. So it wasn't too long before feelings of discontent and dissatisfaction began to show, especially after I had refused to have a Muslim wedding.

One of the main frustrations I felt whilst we were living with Hamid's parents, was that Hamid never discussed any plans with me that concerned our life together; instead, he discussed these with his parents. So decisions were made and directions taken that affected me directly but that I had no say in or control over. This, eventually, caused a great deal of anger and resentment in me as I felt my value as a person and a wife was being undermined.

Me in Iran in the early 1970s

CHAPTER FIVE

RHUDBARAK

Iranians consider a guest to be a 'gift from God' and they go to great lengths and expense when entertaining, to make sure that the fare is abundant and excellent, that guests are happy, well catered for, kept amused and are comfortable. My arrival seemed to create a sense of excitement among the wider family and friends and so we spent a lot of time socializing with them as they were eager to meet Hamid's new wife—though, there were some who weren't so happy about him choosing a wife outside the family—and a foreign one at that.

He kept our marriage a secret when he returned to Iran and aunts were quite hopeful that he would choose to marry one of their daughters. But to everyone's surprise he announced one day that he already had a wife who would be arriving from Britain very shortly. All the hopes and plans they had made over the years to merge families and wealth, were scuppered, and, as you can imagine, I was not the 'flavour of the month' to them when I arrived. So, not everyone was pleased to meet me, but they got used to me in time, and I managed to adapt to those less friendly situations. Generally, though, most people were very kind and friendly, and very generous towards me, and I enjoyed being with them.

When I first arrived in Iran, Hamid told me not to venture out on my own, but to take the car and the driver with me. This made me afraid to go out alone, but one day, after an angry outburst, I stormed out of the house and just started marching off without thinking where I was going or whether I'd be safe. I walked for a long time at quite a pace in the midday heat, and became even more angry as drivers started honking their horns at me and slowing down as they drove past. Eventually, I became aware that a car was following me. I looked round and saw Asdollah at the wheel and Hamid sitting in the back. He told me to get into the car, which I did, and we drove back home. This incident prompted me to start thinking about moving away from Hamid's parents and getting a home of our own, but this didn't happen for quite a while. So the next few months were spent going to concerts at Rhudaki Hall; taking trips at weekends to the family's *bagh* (orchard) out in the countryside of Jabon, where the temperature was much cooler; or staying at a friend's villa, surrounded by orange trees, by the Caspian Sea.

One of my favourite places, more inland in the Caspian area, was a place called Rhudbarak, where a village of the same name nestled between lush, hilly forests. Higher up, steep rocks, sometimes shrouded in mist, challenged men to climb them, but not without an experienced guide.

We usually went to Rhudbarak in the summertime to escape Tehran and the heat of the city. It was cooler there and staying in the village with Mash Safar's family gave us the opportunity to sample village life first-hand. Mash Safar, our host, was a small, nimble man with sharp facial features and a pointed nose. He always wore a brown deer-stalker hat with a feather stuck at the side in the band. He was thin and wiry, dressed in a checked, flannel shirt, and knee-breeches with elasticated braces. Mash Safar had an international reputation for his mountaineering expertise and European climbers from Switzerland, Germany and France had hired him to guide them up that precipitous climb, especially in winter-snow and ice.

I loved coming here to the summer-green hills where cows and sheep wandered, and willow branches dangled lazily in the flowing river, and where the unhurried, yet, purposeful pace of village life kept time with the seasons; daylight and night-dark, sunshine and rain, the heat of summer and the cold of winter. All the difficulties I'd experienced in Tehran, so far, seemed a million miles away when we were here: nature and the simple way of life made us forget everything in the city. But Mash Safar and his family were always eager to hear news of what was happening in Tehran and after showing us our room, he would scurry off to the *samavar*, returning with a round, metal, painted tray on which steaming *estacahns* (small glasses) of *chai* slid in his rush to show his hospitality.

Have you seen so-and-so's latest film? He would ask excitedly. *And have you heard this new song by Googoosh?* (A pop singer)

Then, clicking his fingers rhythmically, as Iranians do, he would turn up the volume of the small, pale-blue, portable radio and begin singing along with exaggerated expression to make us laugh. His young sons, who always came to welcome us, joined in as they sat around the edge of the *soffreh* (tablecloth on the carpet). We sat on the floor talking, laughing and listening to each other, while I tried to master the art of preventing the white lump sugar, clamped firmly between my front teeth, from dissolving too quickly, as I sipped the strong, black tea. I loved the way they made me feel welcome and the way their happy, friendly children tried to help this *kharnoom ingilisee* (English lady) understand their dialect.

Then, settling down for the night, the quiet darkness interrupted occasionally by a distant dog's barking, sleep would overtake us and we drifted off into another world.

At the cockerel's call the following morning, we'd open our eyes to shards of bright sunlight piercing the darkened room. We'd leap up and begin piling the *dohshaks* (thin mattresses) we'd slept on, in a corner to make way for the *sofreh*. A tray of hot tea and breakfast would already be waiting for us when we opened the door. Fresh, crispy *barbari* bread with butter and home-made jams; locally sourced honey; boiled eggs; home-made *panir*; hot, black tea;

hot milk; slices of watermelon and dates, accompanied by lots of chat, was always a good way to start the day. All meals here were eaten cross-legged on the floor around the *sofreh.*

Then, after breakfast, everyone got themselves organised to go walking in the beautiful valley at the foot of the rocks for the day. Food—especially melons and drinks—were the most important items to take, so that when we found a particularly lovely place, we would stop, usually by the river, and have lunch. Afterwards, we'd lie back and doze in the shaded warmth of the afternoon sun, and listen to the sounds of nature as the river rushed on. Birdsong and the odd fly's buzz overhead were unable to stir us.

Later, we'd resume our walk after bundling everything back into our rucksacks, and continue along the worn, earth path for a couple of hours or so before turning back. It was important to keep track of time in the afternoon, as darkness quickly descended around seven in the evening, and it was better to be back in the village where we'd be safe from harm. On our return, we could hear Mash Safar's daughter-in-law, Effat, calling out to the hill behind their house, and singing little songs in a loud voice. When we asked what she was doing, she replied:

I'm calling the cows in from the hills for the night. And, sure enough, down they came, one by one, and settled in the field nearby.

Another day, before breakfast, we watched the women

The river running through Rhudbarak

Keeping cool in the shade

Two little girls from Rhudbarak

The Caspian area

making *nan e lavosh* (flat, unleavened bread) in the *tandoor* (a round, clay oven, alight with burning coals, set deep into the ground) in a separate building at the rear of the house. A team of three women worked together to produce their daily bread: one made the dough, another baked it in the *tandoor,* then the third woman collected the cooked bread and laid it on a clean cloth inside the room. It was of great interest to me because I hadn't seen this type of 'oven' before, yet in Iranian villages it was quite common. The people worked hard doing their daily chores but seemed happy and carefree, although some women appeared unwell and tired, and suffered after giving birth. Effat was one of these women. Whether this was due to women choosing more traditional methods of having children by relying on the local women to act as midwives, rather than having their babies delivered in hospital, I'm not sure.

Another skill some of the women had here was weaving Persian rugs. Carpet weaving was very lucrative and a skill that raised a family's income considerably. As we meandered along the village path, at times through mixed flocks of sheep and goats shepherded by young boys, ten or eleven years old, and their faithful dogs, we came across women sitting cross-legged on the veranda outside their homes, deftly threading, pulling and crimping woollen tufts into the Hessian warp on the carpet frame. Sometimes, two or three people in a row worked together, each following a paper section of pattern showing both the design and colours to use. These patterns were often indigenous to the area, and some had been used for generations.

The people of Rhudbarak were a fine example of community life and how well they worked together, using all the skills their ancestors had taught them to make a living—though some men worked outside the village driving taxis or small vans, etc. They knew how to survive the harshness of the very hot, summer weather, and the very cold, snowy winters, and how to be thankful. Some younger ones, though, seemed attracted by the idea of living and working in Tehran.

FURTHER DOWN FROM RHUDBARAK WAS THE CASPIAN SEA, and the lush, dark-green beauty of forests further in the distance. What a contrast it was to the hot, dry, dusty climate of Tehran. Those warm, summer nights spent there in the company of good friends and good food were times I remember with a longing to be back there again. The bright-green cricket's shrill chirp in the orange grove in the quietness of the night, and the odd light or two shining on the darkness of the sea in the distance, gave a sense of 'all's well here', all, except the gradual decline of closeness between Hamid and me.

When we were with others he rarely spoke to me, but seemed to enjoy conversations with those around him – making them laugh, and singing and dancing. During these times Farsi was the predominant language, still much of which I didn't understand, and as time went on, this became a powerful tool of exclusion

Hamid used against me, to gain control over both me and every situation we were in together. So back in Tehran after one of these trips, I enrolled on a Farsi language course in the hope that this would solve the problem of feeling 'left out' in situations. All went well at the beginning, but Hamid soon grew tired of my asking his help over difficulties I had with grammar and pronunciation, and told me not to bother him. Neither did he encourage me to speak Farsi. But gradually, as time went on, we established friendships with people who were bi/tri-lingual, who would speak to me in English. But, little by little, I learned enough Farsi to speak to my in-laws, and to venture out to do the shopping; and in time, picked up enough vocabulary, mainly from local shopkeepers and through daily interactions with the general public, to get by. Hamid's job at that time was to supervise and teach English as a foreign language to classes of air cadets at the Air Force Academy in Tehran, and I suppose that, after a day's teaching sometimes reluctant, young students, he was pretty tired when he came home and didn't want to be bothered with my language difficulties.

CHAPTER SIX

A SPECIAL INVITATION

During my first months in Tehran, my parents-in-law received an invitation from the Imperial Court to attend a special celebration of 2,500 years of Iranian monarchy, to be held in the ancient grounds of Persepolis, near Shiraz, south of Iran. They were unable to attend this function due to another official engagement there on the same day, so my father-in-law arranged for Hamid and myself to go instead. So on a bright, sunny and very warm day, early in the morning, we all boarded a special plane filled with military personnel and their spouses, and flew directly to Shiraz airport. We then travelled to Persepolis the following day as we had been given special permission to visit Persepolis the day before the event.

On arrival, my father-in-law was greeted by an army guide whose job it was to show us round the ancient ruins and, in particular, the accommodation where the Shah's guests would be staying during the celebrations.

We began our tour by briefly scanning the enormous grounds where the time-worn summer palaces of Cyrus the Great, King Darius, Xerxes, and Artaxerxes had been, and where the conqueror, Alexander the Great's feet sped as he captured the Persian Empire. The lofty, vertically rib-carved stone columns with large, carved and delicately patterned bases stood interspersed between the geometrically aligned remains where columns had once stood, giving an impression of palatial grandeur. Beautifully carved stone relief depicting processions of envoys from Media, and Mede and Persian guards, and shepherds leading sheep to sacrificial death, lined a high wall beside a flight of wide, low-level, stone steps which, long ago, kings and noblemen carefully ascended and descended on horseback.

But on this day, two thousand five hundred years later, as *we* ascended the steps, a sand-coloured snake—head raised a good foot high—silently slithered down to greet us! Our courageous guide ran forward, brought up his leg and crashed his boot down on it, continuing to stamp on it until it was dead. We were all immensely grateful, to say the least! As we continued up the steps I kept looking around to see if there were any more snakes, which somewhat dampened the wonder and romanticism of the place. But as we reached the top, and looked through and beyond the columns, our attention was drawn away to a number of smart, circular, sand-coloured tents nestled in the background. Our guide informed us that these were to accommodate all the heads of states attending the celebrations, so we headed towards them, enthusiastically. The guests were not due until the following day and the tents were empty, so our guide offered to show us round the tent Mrs Indira Ghandi would occupy during her stay. Stepping inside this beautifully furnished tent was a real eye-opener, and was like stepping into a modern, purpose-built apartment with solid partitions between rooms, and a separate section with a small kitchen for a servant-in-waiting. We then moved on to the huge, striped, blue and sand-coloured banqueting marquee, with its wide, dark-blue canopy, providing shelter from the scorching heat over the entrance. Here, in the days ahead, the Shahanshah would lavish wonderful and extravagant feasts on his guests. We marvelled at this amazing construction and the idea behind it at the time, but after the event, the extravagance of the celebrations became a political talking point.

Back in Shiraz that evening, we ventured out into the warm darkness to visit the gardens where the tomb of the great fourteenth century Iranian poet, Hafez, lay. The flickering, candle-lit grounds are a must-see for romantics, where love, and a timeless serenity seemed to be, in the twinkling darkness, among the dead.

Many Iranians go there to consult the wisdom of Hafez when they have a secret wish, or are facing difficulties. First, they whisper their request to Hafez, then, randomly open a book of his poems to reveal the answer from the poem on that page, which they then interpret and consider to be the direction to take.

THE FOLLOWING AFTERNOON A SPECIAL COACH arrived to take us back to Persepolis for the Celebration parade. When we arrived we were guided off the coach, through the security check, then to our seats. We sat among the throng of people taking in the scene, excited, yet unsure of what to expect. The first thing we noticed in the distance was armed guards dressed in Achaemenian military uniform and evenly spread out on top of the high wall that went the whole length of the parade area, which was huge. (The Achaemenian dynasty ruled from 599-330 B.C. and was the period that marked the beginning of the Persian Empire.)

In front of the wall was a high platform where the Shahanshah and his guests sat in the afternoon sun.

Numerous heads of state had been invited so security was very tight. Through my binoculars, and to the distant left, I could see the Shah sitting chatting to Prince Philip and King Hussein of Jordan. Anwar Saddat, King Carlos of Spain, Mrs. Indira Ghandi, King Olaf of Sweden, Princess Ann, and Henry Kissinger were others I recognised. There were also many I couldn't identify because I couldn't see them clearly.

Like most things in Iran, events rarely began on time. The chattering spectators began to fidget as they waited in the heat. Then suddenly, without any warning, a loud fanfare pierced the air and silenced the crowd. The Shah stood up and welcomed everyone to this very special occasion, then commanded the parade to begin.

A powerful musical composition, specially written for the

celebration and played on replica, period instruments, grabbed our attention. The sounds were astonishing and aroused a high level of eager curiosity about what was to follow, but before we could catch our breath, the Achaemenian army in all its splendour was marching in front of us, wonderfully dressed in beautiful, dark-blue robes trimmed with red and blue patterns. Tall, pleated, matching-blue hats rested on their flowing, black hair; earrings, black beards and shields all glistening in the sun. Gasping with excitement, everyone stood up, some clambered unsteadily onto their seats, to see this magnificent, majestic, military-disciplined, gorgeous body of men go by!

Next came the Parthian soldiers in a huge battle tower pulled by enormous oxen. The animals' legs were almost flat against the ground as they strained with all their might to pull this heavy weight. It was so dramatic—we were all spellbound.

The Sassanid Navy followed them. Dozens of sailors rowed their oars in unison to the beat of a drum in the galley of an enormous battleship, as solemn men paced the deck waiting for a signal from the lookout who watched for enemy ships, high up in the crow's nest.

On it went, through each dynasty of 2,500 years of Iranian monarchy, each period depicted by the style of uniform worn and weapons carried by the soldiers, right through to the modern-day army of the Pahlavi Dynasty and its mighty display of military weapons.

What a thrill it was to be there to witness this electrifying extravaganza, a once-in-a-lifetime sensation, never to be forgotten.

Deeply impressed, you can imagine how often we recalled memories of our trip to Persepolis, in particular, the spectacular parade. But the extravagance of the Celebrations became a topic that provoked much discussion at dinner parties back in Tehran, sowing seeds of discontent. Little did we know, at the time, that before the end of the decade, the Shah would be deposed and his government toppled from power.

Perhaps, as the Shah stood in all his splendour among the ruins of the palaces at the parade, his dream was to revive the Persian Empire, whilst unaware that he was being prepared by a Greater Power for the downfall of his own dynasty and the end of monarchical reign in Iran. And perhaps Farid Ud-Din Attar, the 12th century Persian mystic poet, unknowingly, but aptly, portended these events in his poem: *The Conference of the Birds,* when he wrote:

This universe will fade – this mighty show
In all its majesty and pomp will go,
And those who loved appearances will prove
Each other's enemies and forfeit love.

(Translated by Afkham Darband and Dick Davies, 1984)

CHAPTER SEVEN

AN UNEXPECTED TURN OF EVENTS

In 1976 the construction of the eight-floor apartment block, where we later lived, was completed, and, in due course, we moved into our new home on the sixth floor. This very generous gift was given to us by Hamid's parents who, not only provided us with a new home, but also with new cars in succession. Life was easy for us financially, and meeting up with friends for lunch at the Sheraton or Intercontinental Hotels, or having my hair done at the Hilton, were regular events.

It was during this period that my parents contacted us to say that they would like to visit us the following spring. This was good news for me because familial company was very much with my husband's family, which, at times, made me feel alienated from my own culture and sense of family. This also affected my sense of who I was—my individual identity—particularly when things were not going too smoothly between me and Hamid. So I really looked forward to them coming over and to having conversations

View from the balcony of our apartment

A park in north Tehran where people would stroll in the cool of the evening

At Dizin Ski Resort

Mum and dad sunning themselves as we skied

in English-English and feeling the familiarity of my parents being around, despite our dysfunctional relationship.

Early the following March they arrived at Tehran Airport laden with all sorts of goodies that were 'British': chocolates, Liquorice Allsorts, pork pies(!) and a multi-coloured tank top my mother had knitted specially for me - in hideous colours! (I never did wear it and she was most upset about that). But as the Iranian New Year (March 21st) began to creep up on us, there was a sense of excitement about the holiday and what the New Year would bring. We planned to take them to Dizin ski resort for a few days after the new year celebrations, and, there were also the obligatory '*mehmoonies*', mostly with my in-laws, who were very gracious to them - bless them.

Our time at Dizin was one of the most enjoyable times we ever spent with mum and dad, and the weather couldn't have been better. Brilliant sunshine on slopes that had been relentlessly skied on by droves of enthusiastic skiers since the season began, now showed patches of earth and new growth in response to spring's warmer temperatures.

During the day Hamid and I would go off skiing, leaving mum and dad to potter at their own pace. Eventually, we'd spot them soaking up the sun in their deckchairs outside the café halfway down the mountain, clad in Fair-Isle sweater —sleeves rolled up—and matching bobble-hats, hand-knitted by mother, of course. Later we returned to the warmth and comfort of our chalet where hot food, showers and a log fire soothed our aches and pains in the evenings.

Towards the end of their trip, I noticed that dad was getting a bit snappy, so when the time came to say *goodbye*, I wasn't too unhappy about them returning home. Little did I suspect that I, too, would be returning home to Britain just four weeks after they left, to attend dad's funeral.

Was it the flight that caused him to have a heart attack? I sobbed over the phone to my sister in the early hours of the morning.

No, no it wasn't, she said in a comforting tone. I handed the phone to Hamid and buried my tear-stained face in the deep down of the pillow.

I returned to Britain with very mixed emotions. The sadness of knowing that dad had died just before he was due to retire, was huge, as was knowing that I'd never see him again. But, also, mixed emotions because my relationship with Hamid was deteriorating.

I remained in Britain for the next five months which meant I was able to be with my mother and the rest of the family to comfort and be comforted. It also gave me time away from Hamid to weigh up our situation. But I found that, even though I was suffering in my marriage, I still loved Hamid very much and wanted things to work out well between us, to *enjoy* our relationship and be happy together.

I had discovered a couple of years before that I was unable to have children. This was a big blow for Hamid's family, especially because, since the death of their elder son, Habib, they were expecting us to provide them with a grandson to carry on the family name. During this time, Hamid's relatives and friends kept asking:

Batché nemikhi? (Don't you want children?) Or: *Yedooneh pessar beddeh modar-e-Hamid. (Give Hamid's mother a boy.)*

This was repeated so many times after that, that I became quite nervous and distressed when with guests, as I knew that at some point, the topic of our childlessness would arise in front of everyone. To them, there was nothing personal about it, this was a social must! I began feeling very inadequate both as a wife and a person because I wasn't able to 'perform my duty' and because I knew that I had lost my husband's 'favour'. In fact, I was beginning to lose hold of the person I was as the dominant culture of the Iranian way of life took hold of me, and with that a deep sadness began to fill my heart because of the hardened attitude about this very private and sensitive issue. I felt I was no longer accepted for the person I was.

So now I had two big, black marks against me. One for my refusal to have a Muslim wedding when I first arrived in Iran, and the other for my inability to have a child. I felt very alone and unloved, particularly by my husband.

ONE DAY THE PHONE RANG.

Hello Bobbi, it was Hamid. *I've got a ticket to come over in two weeks' time.*

I didn't know whether to be happy because I'd be seeing him soon, or sad because of thinking there would be no change in his attitude when we were together again. But arrive he did and with various gifts for the family. He said that his father had told him to come to Britain to take me back to Iran, and within a week we were on a plane travelling to Tehran, although, when I got there, there was another surprise waiting for me.

I've enrolled on an MBA residential programme at the Iran Centre for Management Studies starting in a few weeks' time. It's a one year intensive course where all students are required to stay on campus for the first two terms. He could have knocked me down with a feather. He continued: *But you'll have the car and you can phone me, if you need to(!)*

Yes, it was a good opportunity for him because it was a top-notch Management Centre, affiliated to Harvard University, and whose lecturers were mostly academics from Harvard. Also, his mother was paying for it all, so everything seemed perfect—to him. But, why did he want me back in Tehran if he was going away for a year?

The course literature stated that:

Along with the quality of both Faculty and students and the meaningful duration of the program, it is the detachment from the responsibilities of firm and family in the academic environment that gives the ICMS program its unique quality.

What was I supposed to do while he was away? He already knew that I lived quite a restricted life, and had he not yet realized that the only reason I was in Tehran was to be with him? The decision had, again, been made behind my back and I was just expected to fall in with the plan. Needless to say, I was hurt and angry that everything had been 'signed and sealed' without consulting me. But then, he seemed to enjoy springing surprises on me where he knew I was unable to do anything about them. I couldn't even leave the country and go back to Britain without his permission.

THE CENTRE WAS ESTABLISHED IN 1970 and its design was based on that of early theological schools, yet modern, and with very pleasant gardens set within sixteen acres of land north of Tehran. The concept, curriculum and academic standards of ICMS were modelled after the Harvard Business School, and its aim was to provide training exclusively for upper management positions both in business and government. The chairman of the board of trustees was Prince Abdorreza, the Shah's brother: other board members included government ministers and high-profile businessmen.

It was a beautiful September morning in 1977 when I drove Hamid to the campus. We said our goodbyes and I returned home to our apartment. It seemed empty already and although I'd spent periods on my own at home when he went mountain-climbing, etc., I was used to him not being around for only a day or two, and mostly, on Sundays when I went off to church. This new period was going to be the longest time I had lived in Tehran without him.

Come and stay with us, don't stay on your own, his mother insisted over the phone, which was kind, but I didn't want to be with her - I wanted to be with him.

But as the weather started warming up the following year, things seemed to get better. As a student's spouse I had access to some of the campus facilities and in time, became a regular visitor on sunny afternoons to the turquoise-blue, outdoor swimming pool. I looked forward with a sense of freedom to popping my salmon-pink bikini in my bag and driving up Vanak Parkway, north of Tehran, to spend time reclining in the shade of a tree beside the glistening pool, or taking a dip in the warm water. Often I was the only person there, except for a waiter who sauntered over in the heat of the afternoon with a tray bearing ice-cold lager, Seven-Up, and nibbles which he placed neatly on a table beside me, then flip-flopped back to his kitchen. A lager shandy was a 'must' on a hot summer's day, there, and gradually, as nature hummed its afternoon song and the air grew warmer, I began to relax. A quietness crept into my troubled heart as I began to let go of my problems by the shimmering water. Sometimes, if Hamid was free and knew I was at the pool, he'd come over and join me for a while, but as he was mostly accompanied by his classmates, we had little time alone together.

One time during the winter I phoned him.

We were given the day off yesterday so a group of us went skiing at

Dizin, he said cheerily. My heart began to sink as he continued: *The snow couldn't have been better.*

Why didn't he ask me to join them, I thought? It seemed ICMS's *'detachment from the family'* was having an effect.

ONE AFTERNOON I WAS SITTING AT HOME LISTENING TO MUSIC, when I became aware of something resting on the bottom of the window frame outside. I paid little attention to it until it began moving; then it stopped. I went to investigate and found a fascinating and curious insect perched very firmly in the metal groove across which the window slid open and closed. I looked at it for a long time trying to figure out what it was, never having seen anything like it before. It was about six or seven centimetres tall, and light grey in colour, with definite facial features; eyes that blinked, and a clearly defined mouth; slim, flat wings pressed either side of its body, and two legs-—thick as cherry stalks—with peculiar, cupped feet that looked like tiny grey, round-toed boots. No other arms or legs were visible and it stood upright, with one eye on me and the other looking ahead. Now, remember, we were on the sixth floor and quite high up for an insect to fly.

Plucking up courage, I opened the window enough to poke at it with a ruler and try to dislodge it, but it wouldn't move. I tried again, it moved very slightly this time, but I quickly drew back my hand in fear and shut the window. I watched it through the glass, waiting for it to fly away, but it settled back in the groove where it remained for a very long time. As the afternoon wore on, I kept checking to see if it was still there, and, yes, it was. It looked like, what I thought might be, a giant locust. Now, in hindsight, I wonder if it might have been a messenger, portending things ahead in our lives that we were not expecting.

When I got up the next morning it was gone.

AT LAST GRADUATION ARRIVED and with a flurry of excited activity. Invitations were received, together with the warning: *and don't be late,* from Hamid, and parents-in-law, myself, the chauffeur, and appropriate apparel for the event, were organised.

The open-air ceremony in the garden was held in the evening as the sun was setting. The air in Vanak was slightly cooler than that at home and this made the evening more enjoyable. Speeches were said, both the Centre and the students were praised, names were read out in succession, and the graduates went forward to receive their diplomas, with a handshake from Prince Abdorreza. It was a very special evening in a lovely setting, and as names were being read, I glanced over at the distant trees' silhouettes against the changing, streaky-amber and then grey sky, as I waited to see the day's sun disappear.

After the ceremony it was time to party the evening away by the softly-lit swimming pool. Everyone was happy and singing and dancing, enjoying the freedom of successfully completing the course, whilst anticipating an exciting future. Things can only get better, was what they might have been thinking, but in the distance,

Hamid at ICMS

Receiving his MBA award from Prince Abdorreza

the rumblings of political discontent and growing unrest were being heard at the other end of the city.

Hamid managed to secure the post of Marketing Strategist with an international company upon leaving ICMS. It was a good company to work for and the work challenged both his creativity and imagination to develop new ways of thinking. It was very different from his work at the air-force academy where he taught English. He was popular with his colleagues—of course—and quite a few of them became very good friends as time went on.

One day reports of anti-government protests by students on Tehran's university campus came over the air waves as we ate breakfast. The Prime Minister didn't seem too perturbed by these protests and he was quoted as saying that it was a natural and healthy way for students to let off steam. However, within a short space of time, this good-natured acceptance of what was happening began to change as students increased in number outside the campus on the streets. The rest of us in the capital were glued to the TV and radio waiting for the next news bulletin as government warnings to the students to stop their protests were now being issued. There was a short lull in activity at this point and Tehran buzzed with speculation at the unknown. Then the students came back again, this time bolder and louder. More people were joining them, their 'voice' was getting stronger.

The police were out on the streets now telling them to disband and go home, but the people kept on shouting

Demonstrations in Tehran that led up to the Revolution

and marching.

As days went by, there were clashes between demonstrators and the police and people got hurt. Someone threw a petrol bomb and set fire to a shop doorway, then another, and another. Riot shields, helmets and batons were not enough to protect the police anymore, so the army came out onto the streets with rifles. Hundreds of people now joined the demonstrators shouting *Maarg baar Ámerica (Death to America)* and in days to come, effigies of Uncle Sam and Jimmy Carter were hung by their necks from prominent places in the city and set on fire. Troops were now shooting warning shots into the air, and at first, people scrambled to safety. But as the situation worsened and it was clear that there was no going back, troops began firing shots at the demonstrators, filling us all with terror. Tanks suddenly appeared on the streets and a bloody battle ensued. Many people were killed and many were wounded.

The ordinary things of life like shopping, going for a walk in the evening, visiting family or friends became minimal and had to be carefully planned for safety's sake. I remember having to go out one day—always by car now and with a driver—and, though going wasn't a problem, coming back was. We hit the problem at the intersection of Shah Reza Avenue and Kakh Avenue. Huge crowds filled the streets and were demonstrating with great passion along Shah Reza Avenue; soldiers were responding with bullets. The atmosphere was electrifying and people ran in all directions.

Glass and all kinds of debris littered the streets. Asdollah, the driver, eyes all over the place, saw his chance and sped across the wide dual carriageway, hand fixed on the car's horn whilst trying to avoid driving into the demonstrators. The sound of rifle shots filled the air.

Get down, get down, he insisted.

I dived face down on the back seat and Asdollah ducked behind the wheel as much as he could. Someone ran in front of the car.

Get out of the way, Asdollah shouted, *let me through.*

The man ran off shouting slogans against the Shah and America, and, suddenly, the way was clear. We sped up the road as fast as we could and drove into the parking area beneath our apartment block.

Phew, I thought, *that was close!*

Uttering a hasty goodbye to Asdollah, I jumped out of the car and ran to the lift which brought me up to the safety of my home.

But the people were relentless and in the days ahead, as anarchy and violence intensified on the streets, mobs began gaining the upper hand. Widespread strikes immobilised airports, oil refineries, and the Central Bank. The British Embassy was set on fire as anti-western feeling came to a head, and Jaffar Sharif-Emani was appointed Prime Minister by the Shah in the hope that he would be able to quell the violence across the nation. But he was unable to do so and resigned his post soon after his appointment.

It was then that a new curfew from the hours of 9pm to 5am came in to force to try to curtail anti-government activity.

CURFEW WAS AN INTERESTING IMPOSITION. Everything came to a standstill in the capital as guards at various checkpoints in the city controlled our movements at night, all, that is, except for a lone dog barking a couple of blocks away. We were still trying to get used to the quietness all around us as, normally, before all the political problems began, people would have been entertaining guests in their gardens, or having wedding parties outside, and singing and dancing, and the city would have been buzzing with activity until the early hours of the morning.

This particular night, though, unable to sleep because of the heat, we lay silently listening to the dog. The barking continued for quite a long time when suddenly, Hamid jumped out of bed, grabbed his small radio and marched out onto the balcony. I waited a while for him to return, wondering what he was doing out there. Then the dog began barking again and a few seconds later I heard a slightly different bark. The dog barked again and this slightly muffled bark followed. So I got up and went to the balcony to find Hamid waiting for the dog to bark again so that he could play back his recording! (He was never a passive listener!) He did this for quite a while before giving in to fits of laughter.

But other nights weren't so funny. Soldiers yelling at people defying curfew rules, followed by rifle shots threatened us psychologically in the quietness of the night. Now when we made our journey to Hamid's parents at weekends, we stayed overnight to avoid punishment, and being 'out after hours'.

This was an interesting, yet frightening time to be in Tehran. For me, as a British subject, both the burning of the British Embassy, and the grounding of all air transport due to strike action, terrified me. I felt completely trapped by a battle I was not participating in. The radio was permanently switched 'on' at this stage and most instructions from the government were read to the nation by very serious newsreaders. Then amongst all this, rumblings of a different kind were felt. One night we were sitting having dinner when I noticed the lamp hanging above the table begin to sway. It took a minute or two to realize that this was an earthquake tremor and while the lamp swayed vigorously now, the phone rang.

Midoonam, maman, balé, chasm, (I know, mum, yes, of course).

Hamid was speaking hurriedly while motioning to me to get out of the flat. He put the phone down, grabbed me by the arm and, together, we leapt down six flights of stairs, alongside everyone else in the building, into the street. (Note to you, dear reader: never get into a lift during an earthquake to avoid being trapped in it, always take the stairs; that's what I was told to do.) People were very frightened and panicking, but once out in the street, we realized that we were still vulnerable to any falling debris! So where was the best place to go to find safety?

Later, we heard on the news that this had only been a

tremor and that a major earthquake had occurred miles away and many lives and homes had been lost.

Adapting to all these disruptions wasn't easy, and all that was happening around us certainly kept us on our toes. Keeping safe was our main priority during this period, and though we tried to live life as normally as we could, while Hamid was still going to the office, as usual, I kept as close to home as possible.

One day I had to go down the road to do some shopping. I cautiously weighed up the situation out on the street before stepping out. The local grocer's was only about a hundred yards away and the commotion sounded further away so I took my chance and went as quickly as I could. Once inside I joined the line of customers and waited. I felt safe there, knowing that the smiling, young man who always served me, was kind and helpful. Then, out of the blue, a voice from behind said in a very unpleasant tone, close to the back of my head:

You foreigners aren't welcome here, why don't you go back to your own country instead of milking ours.

I felt intimidated, but replied: *I can't.*

Why not? he questioned.

Because my husband is Iranian, I answered.

He was stumped for words as he realized that some foreigners were in Iran for reasons other than those he had accused me of. At this point, my bold shop assistant ignored the people in front of me and came to my rescue, bless him.

What can I get you, khanoum?

I bought the tea and hurriedly left the shop feeling upset and afraid. This was the first time I'd experienced any hostility as a foreigner here, and it was enough to make Hamid think that I would be safer out of the country. So arrangements were made for me to travel back to Britain, but this time on a military plane, as all commercial flights had been suspended due to strike action. I felt so relieved to be getting away from the situation, whereas Hamid seemed to thrive on it. He stayed behind in Tehran and I know my leaving Iran released him from worrying about my safety.

CHAPTER EIGHT

ITALIAN SURPRISES!

When the time to leave Iran came, I clambered aboard the plane and found a seat, but instead of sitting in small rows of three or four people facing the front of the plane, passengers sat side-by-side in two long rows opposite each other, and harnessed in. Everyone on the plane was in some way connected with the armed forces and there were lots of mothers with children on that flight who were, no doubt, very glad to be leaving Iran at that time.

The journey was long and the engine was very noisy. The children began to get irritable after a while, but soon fell asleep with a little coaxing from their mothers. Around midnight the pilot announced that we would soon be landing (fortunately, we weren't expected to parachute down to our destination!) and that we should make sure our seatbelts were fastened as landing might be a bit bumpy. So, we obediently followed instructions, and the plane, eventually, touched-down in the middle of an Italian air force base. Little did we know what would be waiting for us once we landed...

The plane came to a halt. Someone said we were near the sea, but it was impossible to see anything in the darkness. We stood up in an untidy huddle, clutching our bags as we waited for the door of the aircraft to open. Men ran across the runway pushing metal stairs which they fixed onto the doorway, and we began shuffling our way forward to disembark. I was somewhere near the centre of the queue wishing it would move quicker, when, without warning, a white van—a Red Cross ambulance, with sirens screaming and lights aflashing—hurtled full-pelt towards us and screeched to a halt at the foot of the steps. The doors flung open and about six men in white medical coats leapt out and motioned to us to get back inside the plane. *What's going on?* I thought. Their faces bore serious expressions as they yelled and waved their arms about, motioning to us to go back. We turned back feeling disturbed and confused because we couldn't understand what they were saying. When passengers, crew and now an additional two Italians in white coats, were back on board, we were told that we wouldn't be allowed off the plane unless we'd had a cholera vaccination.

What?! We all shrieked together. *But there isn't any cholera in Iran at the moment; why do we need to be vaccinated?*

Just a precaution, came the reply.

The protests began.

You mean you want to inject us without any notification beforehand? You could be injecting us with anything, for all we know.

Tempers and anxieties were beginning to show now, especially when we were told:

If you refuse the vaccination, you cannot leave the plane.

MOMMA MIA! Young girls, alarmed at the thought of being injected, fainted; babies screamed as needles pierced their tender skin; mothers fretted as they tried to soothe their children; and the rest of us stood silently in line.

WELCOME TO ITALY!

We left the plane feeling agitated. We had no idea where we were, and there was barely any light as we walked across the runway blindly following our pilot. We arrived at a small, single-storey, brick building where a man in uniform sat behind a desk. He said something to a colleague who sprang to his feet, opened a door opposite the one we had just come through, and guided us out to a taxi rank on a nearby street. We were told that the taxis would take us to a local hotel where we could get a meal and spend the night. This information cheered us up enormously as we were all very tired and hungry by this time (around 1am).

We readily bundled our luggage into the cars, then, cramming ourselves in, seven per taxi, rode, in convoy and at top speed, to the hotel, which turned out to be just a few minutes away. The cars screeched to a halt in front of the hotel door in succession, and the mood lifted as we laughed when someone joked about how like Iranian drivers the Italians were! Relieved to be so close to a meal and some sleep, we clambered out, unprepared for what was about to happen next. Once out on the pavement, we rummaged in bags for wallets to pay the fares. We only had dollars, pounds or Iranian money between us, so a driver suggested the hotel manager might exchange some of that for lira. But when inside the hotel, the manager said that the safe was locked for the night and that it couldn't be opened till morning. At this point, a heated discussion ensued in three languages, until some bright person stepped forward and said that, as we needed the taxis to take us back to the plane the following morning, we could pay for the total journey then. This extinguished the fire. They all agreed and the drivers left.

We turned back to the hotel manager who, by this time, was definitely in control. His only protection was the desk in front of him in the small reception area, but he looked as though he would take on the whole lot of us, if he had to. We crowded round the desk requesting rooms, one after another.

Passport, he demanded.

We each handed over our passports as he signed us in; he then added that they would be handed back to us when we paid our bills in the morning. We had no choice but to co-operate, even though we were unsure as to whether he would keep his word.

Then there was the question of a meal…

I am NOT getting my staff out of bed at one-thirty in the morning to cook you all a meal, he said sharply.

I could see his point but never tell an Iranian there's no food, no matter what time of day or night it is!

How can you not feed us? we cried in unison. *We've been travelling since eight o'clock yesterday morning and not had a proper meal since then?*

That's not my problem, he said.

We began pleading with him.

Just give us something small to tide us over till breakfast.

Breakfast? He repeated, questioningly. *Doesn't your flight leave at six in the morning?*

Yes, we replied.

Breakfast isn't served until seven, he coldly informed us.

Well, that did it! The women lunged forward over the counter towards him airing their angry complaints in Farsi, hands gesticulating every word.

What about our children, someone shouted, *are you going to let them starve?*

At this the manager stepped back and backed down, he was only inches away from them. He must have realized that they were not going to give in, and, after all, he did have the hotel's reputation to consider, so he agreed to prepare food for us.

We trundled off to our rooms, grumbling as we went. The young porter who took my bags was nice and polite, which I appreciated after all the hassle we'd experienced so far in his country. He unlocked the door of my room and placed my luggage just inside against the wall. He smiled, then turned and left. It was so good to be in this quiet room, and to have time to think for myself about what I needed to do next. There was a knock at the door.

We'll see you down in the dining room in about ten minutes, a voice said; it was a fellow passenger.

OK, I replied, and began sorting out my clothes and toiletries.

WE ALL CHATTED HAPPILY DURING DINNER, as sleepy, silent waiters brought dish after dish of food and laid it in front of us, the sight of which, at two in the morning, was very comforting indeed. But by the time we'd finished eating and I was back in my room, I found it impossible to sleep for fear of not waking up in time to catch the plane. Hamid wasn't there to wake me and there was no alarm clock. I felt quite alone at having to cope on my own in this unfriendly place.

Early the following morning, we all managed to assemble at the hotel's reception desk, eager to settle our bills and regain our passports. Aware of the time, we tried to be as co-operative as we could be. Grouch(o), the hotel manager, insisted on being paid in dollars.

Dollars? Help! I only had pounds, but some kind person came to my rescue and exchanged his dollars for my pounds. I suspect I lost out on that deal, but, hey, it enabled me to pay my bill.

The taxis were there on time and waiting for us as we stepped out of the hotel. We were relieved to see them and gladly handed over our luggage which was promptly thrown into the cars' boots. We returned to the airfield as we had left it the previous night - in a speeding convoy. As we arrived, the plane's engine was already running. We jumped out of the taxis as crew members moved swiftly across the tarmac, urging us to hurry up and get on board. We leapt in to action, quickly delving in pockets or bags for money to pay the taxi drivers, whilst crowding round the back of the cars to retrieve our luggage. I was further back and noticed a couple of Iranians were talking (somehow) to the Italians in a very quiet and serious manner.

Na baba. Chegadr? (You're kidding. How much?) Nemeshe, khaily ziade. (It can't be, it's far too much.)

The Italians threatened to withhold our luggage if we didn't pay what they wanted, little realizing that Iranians are expert hagglers, so best not to treat them like that. The drivers tried to get back in their cars as a fracas erupted. (I've never heard people talk so fast!) They attempted to drive off with our luggage but the Iranians blocked their way (Iran 1 – Italy 0). Arms darted in all directions as tempers raged on both sides, then dropped in defeat as neither agreed to compromise (Italy 0 – Iran 0).

Baba jan, ma bayat berim. (Look, mate, we've got to go.)

But the Italians were resolute. The frustration level was rising even more and a small scuffle broke out between the men.

It was at this point that one of the airport staff arrived and spoke to the taxi drivers. They calmed down somewhat, still glaring at the Iranians, then began unloading our luggage onto the tarmac. A sum of money was handed over and we hurried towards the plane. The air was filled with bad language and heated curses on the Italians at the break of what looked like might be a sunny day.

Once inside the plane we quickly found seats and sat down, and as soon as we were strapped in, the plane started moving and roared along the runway as it picked up speed. The men were still angry and it took quite a while for them to calm down. Then, in a lull, someone started to see the funny side of things, saying that the Italians were as tenacious and as good as the Iranians when it came to haggling. Another remarked that they were *so* like the Iranians in temperament it was unbelievable, and everyone started laughing.

High in the sky now, we were cruising through scattered, white clouds, dotted along the pale blue heavens, with not an Italian in sight. We were all very happy to finally be away from our five and half hour (nightmare!) stay in Italy and on our way to Britain.

The journey seemed to fly by (apologies) and in no time at all, we were landing in the U.K. What a relief. Once through the passport check I made my way to a coach station and from there began my journey 'home' to my mother's house.

In the flurry to leave Iran, I had forgotten to let my mother know I was coming over. It hadn't entered my mind that she could be away on holiday or out for the day! Fortunately, she was at home, but before I arrived there I called in at the local newsagent's and asked if I could phone home. Jenny, my youngest sister, answered the call.

Are you OK? We've been watching the news and it all looks pretty grim, she said. *When will you be coming over, mum's quite concerned about you?*

Oh, in about three minutes, I chirped.

Whaat? she shrieked (shrieking is her speciality!).

Yes, I'm in Alan's shop at the bottom of the road - you can come and meet me, if you like.

The deafening clank of the receiver as she put the phone down brought our conversation to an abrupt end. I thanked Alan and left the shop feeling happy. I walked quickly up the familiar street leading to mum's house. In the distance I could see someone running towards me, a mass of auburn, wavy hair bobbing up and down with each stride. It was Jenny. She ran up to me and threw her arms round me, sobbing as she clutched me to her.

We've all been so worried about you, she cried.

CHAPTER NINE

IN IRAN JUST AFTER THE REVOLUTION

My time in Britain passed quickly, but I found that it took a while to re-adjust to peacetime and cheap TV shows. Britain in 1979 was very different from Iran in 1979. Everyone I met wanted to hear what was happening in Tehran, but their interest soon dwindled as they ran out of things to say. It was difficult for me to find something we had in common, because I was fresh out of revolution in the middle-east, living among people who only viewed it from a safe distance on TV. I was very nervous and stumbled and stuttered over my words and blinked a lot – and still do, at times. Every time I heard a loud bang or a car backfire I became fearful, thinking that it was a rifle shooting. At night I lay in bed worrying about Hamid's safety. We were in touch regularly by phone, and then one day, he informed me that the Shah had left Iran and gone in to exile. I was dumbstruck. What will happen to the country now, I thought? He assured me that things were calming down a bit and that he was OK.

Not knowing what to make of it all, I remained in the UK

for the next few months until Hamid came over for a break. During this time, Ayatollah Khomeini had returned to Iran and there was now a certain dress code there for both men and women. So I went shopping for something suitable to wear and found an Indian cotton, pale blue, ankle-length coat, and a huge, matching, soft-cotton headscarf, and in due course, we travelled back to Iran together

We sat in our seats waiting for the plane to take-off.

You'll see a big change when we get back, Hamid said.

I noticed the women seemed a bit reserved as they chatted to each other. I didn't quite understand why they kept turning away when I looked across at them.

You can loosen your scarf now, Hamid whispered. *You don't have to worry about covering yourself up whilst you're on the plane.*

I untied my blue headscarf and undid the top buttons of my coat.

My wife is British, Hamid informed the two women across the way. S*he's been living in the UK for the last few months and now we're travelling back home.*

Another woman asked a question about my Islamic dress.

No, Hamid replied, *she isn't a 'sister'* (a term used for a female supporter of the new regime). *She just wanted to be sure she didn't offend anyone.*

They all breathed a sigh of relief when they realized I wasn't about to tell them off for not wearing their *hejab* (scarf) properly!

The next six hours were spent chatting, eating, reading and snoozing, as people do when on long journeys, until in the darkness of the night the pilot announced that we had just entered Iranian airspace. It was pitch black outside and nothing was visible from the plane's window. The general mood of the passengers began to change and the atmosphere became quiet and sombre. The plane hummed steadily nearer and nearer to a very serious post-revolutionary situation. Iran now had a new, theocratic government and leader. The Shah was no longer in power—he and his family were in exile—and many of his government ministers had been executed.

GETTING THROUGH THE CUSTOMS check took a long time, because the contents of every passenger's luggage had to be inspected. The customs' officials stood behind two rows of counters, each opposite the other on either side of a large, rectangular, brightly-lit room. We all shuffled forward, and in turn obediently opened our bags at the official's request—we had no choice but to comply. Suddenly, the sound of heavy glass breaking as it hit the floor made us all jerk our heads round. A man fled through the exit as the strong aroma of whisky filled the warm air. (Alcohol is forbidden.) A chill ran through my body as I wondered what would become of this man *when* he was caught. What a foolish risk to take at a time like this.

Our bags were finally cleared and as we stepped out into

the airport lounge, Bahram, the family's chauffeur, signalled to us. We were so glad to see him and quickly got into the car and away from this very scary situation.

'HOME' IS SUCH A FAMILIAR WORD, YET, when we arrived there, it seemed quite unfamiliar territory. It was still in the same place - on the same street - but now, the street had a post-revolutionary new name. Huge, black, thick-lettered slogans decorated the neighbouring walls, and although the atmosphere was more relaxed than when I'd left six months before, there was a cautious check in my spirit, my senses sharp.

We tried to live normally but it was hard for me to grasp that the revolution was done and dusted, that the country had a new leader, and that we no longer had the same status we'd had. We had to learn to live life in a different way.

Hamid had collected a pile of daily newspapers while I was in Britain, whose front pages depicted images of the Shah's top men being executed. The first I saw was of Hoveidah, once the Shah's Prime Minister, riddled with bullets and lying in a bloody puddle, flat on the floor, his famous walking stick by his side. I momentarily thought back to happier times when we had seen him on the TV news with the Shah's small daughter skipping by his side. But now, a thick, black, half inch border framed the photograph, with extra-large, thick black lettering announcing his 'just deserts'. This theme continued in paper after paper showing the violent end of the lives of high-ranking officials. Each image was accompanied by judgemental statements decrying their sins. The photographs were so shocking that I became very fearful of what might happen to us because of being connected to the Shah's army through Hamid's father, and it was during this time that soldiers from the new regime walked into my father-in-laws' office, one day, and began searching for and taking away all data connected to the Armed Forces Insurance, of which he was then head. On another occasion whilst at home, my mother-in-law spotted men with Kalashnikov rifles jumping down from the garden wall and running towards the house. They pushed their way inside and began searching for anything that might incriminate Baba. But on both these occasions nothing was found. All documents, etc., that had been taken were returned to him and he was allowed to live freely from then on. His conscience was clear all along, because Baba was an honest man, and respected as such, but they weren't aware of that. And after forty years' service in the Armed Forces, his integrity saved his life: a thought for us all to ponder.

One amazing change that I thought I'd never see in Tehran was when people had motor accidents (which happened there every day). Instead of jumping out of their cars in vitriolic rage and cursing each other, people actually smiled and accepted responsibility. I was speechless the first time I saw it happen! But perhaps it was due to the feeling that they were always under the watchful eye of Ayotallah Khomeini, whose larger-than-life posters hung from buildings everywhere.

WHILE THE U.S. EMBASSY WAS STILL UNDER SIEGE, urgent news reports of Iraqi military aircraft attacking areas in southern Iran began a panic reaction, and once more, the nation was on alert. Air-raid sirens sounded in Tehran every time there was a strike in the south. We were instructed to take cover each time this happened because no-one knew where the Iraqis would strike next.

Hamid was still going off to work each day, and he reminded me, as he left each morning, what I should do if I heard the sirens. We developed a routine at night where, before going to bed, we would place our clothes at the bottom of the bed, next to a bag containing matches, candles, torches, sandwiches and drinks, in case the sirens went off. The small transistor radio was left switched 'on' all night. One night I was woken up by Hamid saying:

Quick, get up. Go down to the car park, as the sound of the sirens filled the silence.

It was difficult to see where things were because of the blackout. We pulled on our clothes, picked up the bag, and ran as fast as we could out of the flat, down the six flights of stairs and down the ramp to the basement car park which was on two levels. We crouched whispering and listening for unfamiliar sounds in the darkness on the lower level, tucked far back in a recess. All contact with what was going on outside was lost as we failed to pick up any radio signal. We had no idea whether troops had reached Tehran or not, so we were as quiet as possible. Some bright spark pretended to be afraid because he thought a cockroach was travelling along his arm, which only added to the tension.

I was ***so*** scared. I kept imagining Iraqi troops, rifles in hand, running down into the car park and finding us huddled together in the dark. The thought of being captured by these men, these unwanted intruders whose language I didn't understand, was unbearable. We had heard on the news how they had shot dead, husbands and fathers; that they had cut open the stomachs of pregnant women and left them to die, and raped daughters in front of their fathers, and wives in front of their husbands. It was terrifying to hear such things and to think that we could be their next victims. It's amazing how the terror of these situations can paralyse your mind at times like these.

When the 'all clear' signal came it was a huge relief after hours of anticipating the worst, and we all scrambled back upstairs to our homes. The rest of that night we lay clinging to each other, our minds troubled, fearful of what tomorrow might bring. The red 'power' light on the radio was covered over as we waited in the blackout listening for the next alert.

Another night we were woken by the building shaking, and thinking we had been hit by a bomb, jumped up, pulled on the clothes at the bottom of the bed and ran to the door. Hamid suddenly stopped.

What's wrong? I asked.

It's an earthquake! He laughed with a sort of relief, then grabbed my hand and we raced downstairs into the street.

It was soon after this that Hamid decided we would be safer out of Iran, and arranged for us to travel to Britain where things were a bit more stable. This must have been one of the most difficult decisions for him to make, because, not only did it mean leaving behind his beloved Iran, but it also meant leaving behind his ageing parents. Even though they had everything they needed, including domestic staff living on the premises, Hamid was now their only son and they expected him to be there for them till their end. I hadn't understood at the time how deep a wrench this was for him - and them - but I do now.

Trying to convince my parents-in-law that leaving was the best course of action was not easy. They made all sorts of objections, some were really emotionally heavy which piled on the guilt, creating a conflict in Hamid's heart that never left. But his mind was made up and so we started sorting out our furniture to sell, books to keep, stuff to take with us, and our travel documents. My Iranian passport had expired and had to be renewed, so this was the first priority because the processing time could be lengthy.

People came and went, some for goodbye suppers, others to buy furniture. Hamid was still working right up to the next to last day until everything was sorted for us to leave. When the day came, a very tearful mother and father stood waving goodbye to us at Mehrabad Airport, and with very mixed emotions we walked through to the departure lounge.

Let me do the talking, Hamid said as we walked to the passport check.

I handed my passport over to the committé guard standing behind the desk. He calmly looked through the new document. Lifting his head and looking me straight in the eye, he asked, in Farsi, how long I'd lived in Iran. I was suddenly terrified.

Eleven...

Months, interrupted Hamid.

The guard looked a few seconds longer than was comfortable. He turned to Hamid and asked more questions, then, looking back at me, spoke in perfect English.

You know I could check your details... He paused for a moment, then said: *but I don't want to spoil your holiday. You can go.*

I was petrified.

Go on, urged Hamid, pushing me forward. Again, my terrified imagination anticipated walking through the swing-doors only to be arrested by armed guards waiting on the other side. I began to panic. What if we *are* arrested and they found out about the length of time I had actually lived in Iran? What would happen to us? We'd heard reports of very severe punishments being given to people for very mild offences, so who knows what they might do to us, particularly because of our military connections with the previous regime. I could hardly breathe. My heart was pounding.

Our luggage was searched, after which we sat for quite a

while waiting for the plane. People were chatting freely as I watched the guards in silence. I was waiting...waiting to be arrested for giving false information. I thought: but it wasn't me who said it, it was Hamid. He knew that I would have told the guard the truth - that I had been there almost eleven years. But it seemed that God had other plans, which included this new passport that contained no information about how long I'd lived there. (At that time, the government was prohibiting foreigners leaving Iran who had lived there longer than eleven months.)

A VERY DAPPER, SMILING PILOT suddenly appeared at the exit door through which I could see our plane standing on the runway. He apologised for the delay and said:

We're ready for you to board the plane now. Please make sure you've got all your bags with you.

We quickly gathered everything up and walked briskly out the door onto the tarmac. I was screaming with terror inside. What if...what if...? We hurriedly climbed the stairs and, once on the plane, found our seats. There was another delay. We sat in silence wondering what was happening. Then the welcome voice of the captain informed us that the problem had been resolved and that we were due to take off.

Please would you fasten your safety belts?

I can't believe it, I whispered to Hamid.

Don't raise your hopes too much, he said, *they can still call the plane back while we're in Iran's air space.*

Those hours flying high above the clouds filled me with the most awful dread—and I'm sure I wasn't the only one who was afraid. I'm also sure that a good many others were 'holding their breath' until the captain announced:

Ladies and gentlemen, we are now flying over Turkey!

Women began loosening their head-scarves and combing their hair, and men began chatting with one another, although no-one was quite sure whether government agents were among the passengers, so I, particularly, didn't feel completely at ease. But hey, the only way was...down from now on - down onto the runway at Heathrow airport!

CHAPTER TEN

A SAFER PLACE TO LIVE

As the plane touched down at heathrow, news came through that arrangements were being made to release the last US Embassy hostage in Iran. We had left the country at war with neighbouring Iraq and arrived in Britain to the nation watching *Dallas* and *Mash* on TV, and enjoying the freedom of peacetime, all in just six and a half hours. What a contrast in cultures, and what an astonishingly short time it took to change our circumstances and way of life!

We stayed with my mother during those first few months, which was not easy for her or us, because we were used to living a very different life-style. So there were the inevitable frictions and cross words, at times.

During this time, I began attending my local church, St. Margaret's, in Aspley—close to home—and found it to be a very lively fellowship. People were extremely kind to me there and many became good friends, as time went on. Our Vicar, the Rev'd Ray Lockhart, and his wife, Jill, were exceptional in the way they helped and supported me. I was completely disoriented when I first arrived in Britain, and found it so difficult to 'fit in' with the way things were done here, having been traumatised by my experiences in Iran. I couldn't cope with having coffee with people, or with being in a friendly discussion group. I would break down crying uncontrollably, or run out of the room away from people. I stammered, blinked continuously, blushed deeply, and felt completely inadequate. It must have been just as difficult for those whose company I was in to understand why I behaved in this way. But God gave me wonderful friends who knew that, whatever made me behave like this, He could heal, and this is precisely what He began doing - although some things took a long time to surface.

I will always be grateful to my friends at St. Margaret's for putting up with me, whatever state I was in. The patience and love they showed, in particular the Minister and his wife, revealed a loving Father-God who wanted to heal the wounds and bring me to wholeness. As I began to receive God's healing, my faith began to deepen. His tender touch on my life was so real and life-changing, that I gradually became more involved in helping others with their difficulties, and was amazed, again, by the wonderful sensitivity of God's love and guidance.

But while all this was going on, a different kind of battle was going on at home. Hamid was looking for jobs in the national newspapers, and kept choosing to apply for posts abroad - again, without consulting me. It was clear he didn't want to stay in Britain, but I needed to stay here at that time, and to be near my family. Eventually, though, he found work with a local company, which helped to settle the problem for the time being.

Having a job meant that we could apply for a mortgage, and in due course, we bought a two-bedroomed, terraced house, about a mile up the road from where my mother lived. It was a nice little house, modern and very light inside, with a lovely view of a very large, and well-kept piece of grass-land at the back, providing a nice, green, open space to look out on to when washing the dishes! We had good neighbours—all senior citizens–who were nice to us but hated each other! So we were stuck in the middle of their acrimonies and silences, and both sides worked very hard to get us to side with them. As we began to settle there and start life together, without mum, we were able to develop a style of life we were more used to which was more Iranian.

We had made lots of friends through the church by this time, and also renewed contact with some Iranian friends we had known before we went to live in Iran, who also introduced us to their friends. Most of Hamid's friends were Iranian and when we all met up, we would enjoy good food, chatting, singing and dancing in the same way we did in Iran. When we met up with our English friends we would have dinner together or go for walks, to concerts, or to see films. Being with our Iranian friends made us very aware of our drop in status. Where they were flourishing, we were starting again and with no-one to fall back on financially. Adjusting to this was getting difficult for us now. Here, nobody really knew the level we had lived at in Iran, except for our Iranian

Back in the UK

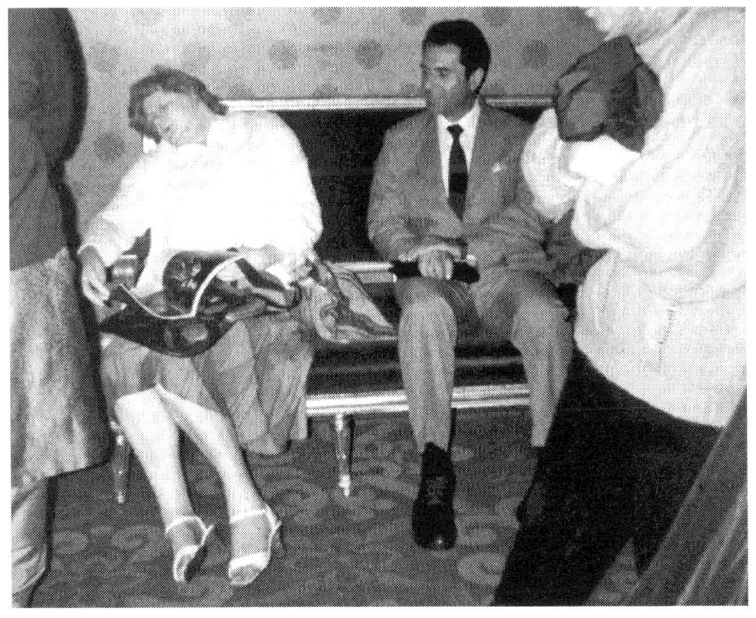

Hamid at Madame Tussauds. Can you spot who's real?

friends, and my mother who had visited us. I was used to living a different and more comfortable way of life among wealthy and more cultured people. Now, living at the other end of the social scale and in a working class area, after having lived away from that for more than a decade, was not easy, even though my roots were working-class. It created a lot of conflict in me when trying to relate to people because I no longer knew where the 'right' level was, and especially, because British culture had 'moved on' and attitudes had changed in the time we had been away. We were caught in the middle of our circumstances, trying to adapt as best we could.

It was during this time that Hamid joined a rock climbing club and started going off with a group of climbers on Sundays while I went to church - much as he had done in Tehran. One day he came home and announced that the group was going climbing in the Isle of Skye and the Cairngorms in a few days' time and that he would like to go with them. Unhappy at the thought of not being asked to go with him, and of spending the next few days without him, I reluctantly said goodbye when the day came.

A couple of days went by with no word from him. He had left no contact number or address, only a rough idea of where they were camping.

The next day the phone rang.

Hello, Bobbi. It was Hamid, he sounded relaxed.

Is the weather good up there, are you having a good time? I responded, trying to sound enthusiastic.

Yes, it's great, couldn't be better. Was his reply.

Where are you phoning from?

Oh, the local pub, it's nice and warm in here, he chuckled.

We chatted for a while then hung up. I felt sad after hearing his voice, I missed him when he was away. But, looking back, I think he chose to behave this way because he objected to my involvement in the church, so it was like a punishment for doing something he didn't want me to do.

The next day the phone rang.

Hello, is that Mrs. Davari?

Yes, I replied.

My name's Sister Hamilton and I'm phoning from the Raigmoor hospital. I just wanted to let you know that your husband's doing fine and that we'll be amputating his wee toe this morning.

W h a a a t?

She understood from my surprise that I didn't yet know about his accident.

You mean you didn't know?

No I didn't. Stumbling over my words and in shock, I continued: *What's happened to him and where is he?*

Oh, I'm so sorry to have to tell you like this. Your husband was brought to the hospital by helicopter a couple of nights ago, after a boulder rolled over the top of a cliff he was climbing and landed on his foot as he tried to shield himself on a ledge underneath. It's damaged all his toes, but four of them, including his big toe, have pins in them and should heal in time. He's really doing fine now, so please don't worry about him, he's in very good hands.

I thanked her for letting me know, and after saying goodbye, sank into the chair, stunned and bewildered.

It took a while for my mind to get in to gear, and when it did, I started panicking. I rang my sister who said I must go to Scotland to be with Hamid. She said they had a friend in Nairn who was a nurse at the very hospital Hamid was at, so she rang her and arranged for me to stay with her. Next I phoned my Vicar and his wife to ask for prayer. They were immensely kind and later arrived at the house with a return train ticket to Inverness. So, with bag packed and everything locked at home, I made my way to the train station where I started the long journey to Scotland. I had to change trains a few times and caught a wrong train heading for Glasgow instead of Edinburgh at one point. Panicking again, I asked a man sitting nearby if I could pick up my Edinburgh connection at the next stop.

Yes, he answered readily, *but you'll need to nip through a little twitchel to the other side of the track.*

He tried explaining the way to me but it just didn't register. He saw my vacant expression.

Don't worry, when we get there I'll hop off the train and show you where to go.

Which he did, then turned quickly and ran back to his train. His kindness really touched me at this particular time when I needed help. Within minutes my train was at the station and I leapt on board checking with someone as I went that it *was* the Edinburgh train, and, thankfully, it was, much to my relief! I found my seat, sorted out my luggage and settled down, letting the train carry me to Edinburgh and then on to the beautiful, open countryside of Inverness.

Denise, bless her, was waiting for me at Inverness Station when I arrived. She promptly took me to the hospital to see Hamid, saying that she'd got special permission from the matron to visit him out of visiting hours.

He caught sight of me as I entered the ward, and I could see right away that he was relieved that the 'game was up' and that he didn't need to keep up the pretence of 'phoning me from the pub' anymore! I was only allowed a brief visit, but that was enough for both of us to cope with as, earlier in the day, he had had his 'wee toe' amputated and now needed to sleep.

The next day I was able to visit at normal visiting times and we were able to talk a bit about what had happened to cause the accident, and about the damage to his foot. His leg, which was elevated and held in place by a rope suspended from the ceiling, was in plaster from the knee down to his foot, and his remaining four toes had steel pins sticking out at the ends. Thick wads of dressing covered the area where his little toe had been and he was clearly in some discomfort. As he lay there, tanned skin against white sheets, he still looked as gorgeous as ever but I was upset to see the terrible damage to his foot. The nurses on his ward were sprightly and cheerful and a good tonic for him, and within a week he was allowed to travel home and attend a local hospital. We took the overnight train which meant he had a bed to lie on for the journey, and we arrived at Nottingham Station early the following morning, where my dear sister and her husband were waiting to take us straight to the Queen's Medical Centre.

Those injuries took a long time to heal and walking was never the same again for him. But as time went on, a walking stick replaced crutches, and eventually, he discarded the stick. He would often complain about having pain in his foot and he had to learn how to manage that.

CHAPTER ELEVEN

A SUDDEN DEPARTURE

During the latter part of 1984, I found a job as a part-time Receptionist at a local medical centre. Hamid was now back at work and we were both locked in to the routines of our timetables and getting on with life. Christmas came and went, and a very chilly January arrived soon after in the new year.

We were snuggled up on the sofa together one evening listening to music when the phone rang. Hamid took the call in the hallway where the phone was. He was speaking Farsi and his voice began to take on a very serious tone; the conversation lasted quite a while before he put the phone down. He sat on the stairs for a minute or two before coming back into the living room. He looked worried and said:

I've got to go to Tehran, mum's had a severe heart attack.

And within twenty four hours he was gone.

It's difficult when serious family things happen in another

country. You can't just nip down the road or even travel to another city in an hour or two to help and comfort people. There was no suggestion of me travelling with him, so I stayed at home and waited for news from him about my mother-in-law. When he arrived in Tehran he was told that she had passed away before they had contacted him. Another awful thing was that the shock had been so great for Hamid's father that he, too, had a heart attack and was in the CCU at a local hospital in Tehran. What a bad time this was for Hamid: his mother's death was immediate and she was buried very soon after, as is the custom in Iran, which meant that the funeral took place before he arrived there. What a sad thing for him to experience while having to spring in to action to look after his father, whose heart attack was bad enough, but not severe. I felt so helpless being thousands of miles away from the situation.

It was a peculiar experience, one where I felt more of an observer after the event than a participant, waiting for the next instalment via the phone, and unable to do anything except pray. But Baba's condition stabilized and he was moved into an open ward.

He was in hospital quite a long time before he was allowed home, but, thankfully, Hamid was able to be there with him in this difficult period. Six months went by and there was nothing else I could do but wait patiently until Hamid could return. My friends at church were wonderfully supportive, and my little job kept me occupied in his absence.

IT WAS DURING THIS TIME THAT A FRIEND told me of someone she knew, who was looking for a good home for a six-week-old kitten.

It's had all its jabs and been checked over, she added.

I'd always been terrified of cats, for some reason, so I could never see me agreeing to have one as a pet. But she was very persuasive, and one day I found myself travelling with her to see what was left of the litter.

Well, who in their right mind could be afraid of a tiny, six-week-old kitten? Little black ball of fur, shiny hazel eyes, tiny patch of beigy fur on her chest, little stick-out ears and whiskers. She strutted round the pen, squeaking as she moved.

Out of a litter of eight, said her owner, *she's the one no-one seemed to want.*

That did it. *Well I want her,* I said, scooping her up in my right palm.

I tried cuddling her but she was too small to cuddle. I told her she was beautiful, she responded with a squeak. I loved her from that very first moment I was told no-one seemed to want her, and she became one of the dearest companions of my life. I named her Zoe because she brought new life into this period of mourning and separation, and I was never again afraid of cats!

We arrived home with all the kitten paraphernalia a new kitten needed: a litter tray with litter; a feeding and milk bowl; kitten food in little packs; a few toys; and a brown and orange large-floral print igloo lined with brown faux fur to keep her warm at night.

The first thing to do, I thought, was to feed her, so I led her to her bowl and she devoured her first meal at her new home in seconds. I then picked her up and placed her in the centre of her litter tray where she stood motionless for a second or two, then started digging down. Delighted by having gained success so quickly in her training in these two most important areas, I started to relax a little and I made myself a cup of tea.

Waiting for the kettle to boil, I thought I'd introduce her to her little igloo bed. I picked her up and popped her inside, half a second later, she popped out. I popped her back in...and she popped back out. I tried again but it was now turning into a game. I tried talking to her:

No, darling, you stay in there and have a little nap, her big, saucer-eyes watching me all the while. Then, out she popped again as soon as I'd finished the sentence. I decided to make my tea and leave her to it, thinking she just might hop in when my back was turned. Instead, after settling in a chair in the living room, in she trotted, no more than four inches high, whiskers fan-like aside her pale-pink nose, her little pink mouth displaying two rows of tiny teeth as she squeaked for attention. What a sweetie! I picked her up and tried stroking the thin fur on her bony back with my fingers. Her little claws kept pulling on my clothes as she walked up and down me. She finally settled in my lap and went to sleep. I daren't move in case she woke up, so just sat looking at her, loving her cuteness. It dawned on me that she'd be dependent on me from now on, and that night, I hardly slept, thinking she might be afraid in this unfamiliar place, away from her previous home. I got up several times to check on her, then, in the end, took her and all the kitten caboodle up to my bedroom so that she wouldn't be alone, and where I could keep an eye on her. (She never did go in her igloo!)

By the time Hamid came back home, she had grown quite a lot and was almost six months old. He was so surprised to see a cat in the house, but he came to love her as much as I did.

THE NEXT FEW MONTHS WERE SPENT checking on Hamid's father, keeping in touch by phone and making sure he was OK. Baba's sister had agreed to look after him for the time being, so we knew he was being well cared for. One day in 1986 the phone rang. It was Hamid's cousin in Tehran.

Your father's been taken to hospital with liver cancer, you must come at once.

After the call, Hamid rushed into the room with the news, saying that we had to go to be with him straight away. Shocked and full of 'ifs' and 'buts' I asked:

What do we do about things here, the house, the cat, our jobs?

Oh, we'll sort all that out. I need to go to the embassy to get our passports sorted and then buy tickets for the soonest flight to Tehran. He ran upstairs and began rummaging in files for the necessary documents. After what he'd experienced over his mother's death, I fully understood the urgency of getting there as soon as possible.

Over the next few days, while Hamid was in London, I contacted family and friends to let them know what was happening. I asked my sister to check on the house from time to time while we were away, and to sort out any bills. A friend volunteered to take care of the cat for however long it took, and we handed in our resignations at work. I went shopping for suitable apparel for an Islamic country and within a matter of days, we boarded the Iran Air flight destined for Tehran.

My family was very concerned about my welfare and had tried to persuade me not to go, but Hamid wanted me to go with him this time, and I agreed with him, because this might be the last time we would see Baba alive.

When we reached Tehran, the first thing we did was go straight to the hospital, where we found Baba half sitting up in bed, with all manner of tubes and equipment attached to him. He saw Hamid first and was overcome with emotion, then he spotted me walking behind, and his tears turned to joy.

Hello, Bobbi. Oh, it's so good to see you!

I felt a lump in my throat as my eyes took in how much he had deteriorated since I had last seen him five years ago. So much thinner—he had always been a rather stout man. His face now yellow and drawn, his eyes cloudy and dull. Dear Baba, I wish I knew what to do.

We all chatted for quite a while until he became too tired

to cope with any more. So we said we'd see him in the morning and left the hospital to make the journey up to the foot of the mountains, to *Shemiran*, to Baba's apartment.

The next few days were spent going to the hospital and just spending time with him. Hamid, poor thing, was busy all the time trying to sort out Baba's business concerns in the midst of everything else. But in the evenings, we were able to visit Iranian friends and relatives, which was really nice for me after not seeing them for such a long time.

Then Baba was allowed home from the hospital, but that only lasted a couple of weeks. He became so weak he had to be re-admitted and on his arrival was taken straight to theatre for emergency surgery, so we stayed with him in hospital that night. An extra bed was brought into his room so that we could be with him and monitor him. He wasn't allowed to eat or drink anything after surgery, but when he became conscious, he kept asking for water.

Later that morning our good friend Nadir popped his head round the door.

Salaam alekoum. His voice was warm and concerned.

I've just given some blood for Baba, he said.

Hamid was glad to see him and as they chatted, I could see Hamid's spirit lift a little. Nadir said he wanted to stay for a while so Hamid told me to go home and get some rest. I went over to Baba and said I was going home for a while but would be back later that afternoon. He nodded weakly, then something made me pause. I looked at his yellow, cloudy eyes.

He's dying, I thought.

I began praying for him quietly in the Spirit. Then, as I prayed, his head started to rise up from the pillow and he began making a long sound like a muffled shout. His eyes were wide open now. Hamid came over and asked him what was wrong but he couldn't answer. He settled back down again and I left the hospital, only to find on my return that Baba had passed away.

Hamid was distraught. I'd never seen him cry before. Nadir, bless him, was a huge support, and after a while, he persuaded Hamid to leave the hospital and go home for some rest, saying that he would take care of the bill and paper work.

There's no point in you staying here now, Nadir said. *Go home and rest.*

THE SILENCE AS WE DROVE HOME was almost tangible; neither of us had anything to say, our words were muted by grief.

An air of gloom hovered about Baba's apartment as we busied ourselves making food that evening. I could see Hamid's helplessness as he came to terms with his inability to change what had happened. I kept trying to be 'helpful' and to comfort him, but he refused to be comforted. He made it very clear from his actions that this was *his* father and that I shouldn't interfere with his grief.

I felt at a loss. He had pulled down all the shutters and there was no way I could get through to him. It hadn't occurred to him that Baba was my father-in-law, that I also loved him and was grieving for him.

The days that followed were devoid of any familiar warmth between us, except when good friends and relatives arrived, bringing kindness with them. The funeral was arranged quickly and on the day when we drove to *Behesht Zahrah*, the cemetery, I could hardly believe what was happening. Whilst the coffin was being carried ahead of us, I could hear the rhythmic sounds of trotting getting nearer. Suddenly, a voice said:

Bebackshid, mazerat mikham. (Excuse me, I'm sorry.)

I turned to see four soldiers carrying a coffin, then another four following with another coffin, then another, and another. They placed the coffins against the side of a wall and went back to collect more.

These are the latest martyrs from the Iraq-Iran war, I heard someone whisper.

This continued for the whole time we were at the cemetery. I was staggered to see the number of coffins carried in that day. The sadness of our party increased as we witnessed so many dead, young men, whose lives had been cut short by the brutality of war.

We quietly moved towards the family grave. Hamid was with his aunt - his father's half-sister - and her family, weeping as he went. I felt so sad for him. It was just over a year since his mother had died and now he was attending his father's funeral.

The grave was covered by a green cloth, with soil heaped

beside it. The pall-bearers stepped forward to place the coffin over the ropes and lower it down, when one of them lost his grip. The coffin fell against the side of the grave forcing off the lid. As the bearers tried to steady the weight, Hamid screamed as Baba's head jolted up in full view of everyone. Hamid was now sobbing uncontrollably. What a terrible thing to happen! I put my arm round his waist to steady him. Others came over to help. The pall-bearers managed to fit the lid back on again and bury the coffin. They later apologised, repeatedly.

Now, looking back, that incident also took the lid off Hamid's emotions where he was 'trying to be brave' and 'hold everything together'. He responded quite naturally, just like anyone would in this situation who had lost a loving parent: there's no shame in that.

I was more than willing to lead him away at the end of the ceremony. We took our time walking back to the car park, along the path beside the other graves there, looking particularly at the photographs of young men who had tragically lost their lives. It made us aware of other people's grief and loss, which, somehow, was comforting, making us feel we weren't alone in our sorrow.

WE RESTED FOR THE NEXT FEW DAYS. I was amazed at how tired we were. Then gradually, Hamid began sorting out the legal side of things because friends and relatives kept dropping in saying that we needed to get started on this. In a way, it wasn't such a bad thing to do because it gave Hamid something else to focus on. Any legal process there usually took ages to complete and there was always a lot of running around attached to it. He was out of the apartment most days from then on, which meant I had time to collect my own thoughts.

Then, back home one evening, the phone rang. Hamid answered it, and as the conversation went on, I realized it was my sister, Marj, calling. I can't tell you how happy I was to know it was her. I think this was my first contact with my family since before the funeral. I waited impatiently for them to finish their conversation so that I could talk to her, but it seemed to go on for rather a long time. Eventually, Hamid came through and handed me the phone. I grabbed it eagerly, and without hesitation began talking to her. We chatted about the family, about the cat, and what was happening over there, and when there was a lull in the conversation she suddenly said:

Has Hamid said anything to you?

What about? I asked.

Oh, er, he's got something to tell you.

What is it? I persisted.

Ask him, Marj replied.

Puzzled by this, but still wanting to hear that familiar voice, I carried on talking until we had nothing more to say. I put the phone down and happily wandered through to Hamid.

Marj says you've got something to tell me.

Oh did she?

Yes, what is it?

Oh, I can't remember her saying anything in particular, he replied, looking at the newspaper.

Are you sure? I questioned again.

Yes. He got up from his chair and left the room.

DURING THE FOLLOWING TWO WEEKS I HARDLY SAW HIM. He was out of the apartment for long periods each day and I had no idea where he was. Some evenings, friends popped round to visit and see how we were getting on, and other times, we were invited out for dinner, and it was at these times, when we were with other people, that I began to notice a guarded kind of behaviour towards me, but thought it might be because of Baba's recent death.

Then one day, Hamid came home at lunchtime. He took hold of me and said:

Come and sit down, I've got something to tell you.

I sat down.

So what is it? I asked matter-of-factly.

He looked down at the floor and started to fidget. I waited.

You remember when Marj phoned and I spoke to her?

Yes...?

Well...well, it's about Penny (one of my older sisters) she's...she's committed suicide. I'm so sorry I didn't tell you before but I knew that I wouldn't be able to get our passports and tickets ready quickly - that it would take at least two weeks before we were able to leave Iran. I thought you'd go crazy if I told you when I first heard from Marj, so decided not to say anything until I had all the travel documents ready for us to leave. Bobbi, tell me I did the right thing, he said desperately.

A volcano of emotion erupted from inside. I screamed and cried, I started yelling, not at Hamid, but at my sister.

Stupid woman, if she hadn't got mixed up with that boyfriend of hers, this would never have happened.

She had been involved with someone else's husband, and seemed besotted by him. She wanted him to leave his wife for her, but that was out of the question.

So what did she do? I screamed: *she killed herself for that creep!* I was so angry, so shocked, so upset: I wanted to hit her for being so stupid, but I couldn't—she had passed on from this world to the next.

The anger and tears went on for a long time that afternoon. My head was aching so much, the pain was becoming unbearable. Hamid was talking to me, trying to calm me down, he made me a hot drink and gave me some painkillers. At the same time, there was a knock at the door, it was Hamid's aunt and her daughter. She took one look at me and said:

Gufti behesh? (Have you told her?)

Baleh. (Yes) he replied.

Then she said an astonishing thing: she told me not to cry now, but to save my tears for when I returned home and was with my family. I was completely baffled by her words.

CHAPTER TWELVE

LIFE GOES ON

By now, about three weeks had gone by when we boarded the plane heading back to the UK. The family had decided to have the funeral earlier, so we were too late to attend it. Hamid stayed for a couple of days then told me he would return to Iran the following day to sort out his father's estate. So, as I grieved with the rest of the family, he travelled back to Iran. This was a really bad time for both of us: Hamid's father's death in Iran, and then my sister's suicide in Britain. My heart was so heavy.

Before Hamid left, we collected the cat from our friend who had taken care of her while we were away. But once home, she didn't want to know us. We tried to coax her, play games with her, even spoil her as a last resort, but she wasn't having any of it. We'd been away for about six months so she may have forgotten about us in that time. It took a few days for her to warm to me, but gradually, that cool aloofness cats have, began to disappear as she responded positively. She might have forgotten us, but after

Me with Zoe

Zoe in her favourite spot by the window

poking her nose into every nook and cranny in the house, she may have remembered that, when she was a kitten, she used to live there.

I was so glad to have her at this awful time. She was such a comfort and filled a huge gap while Hamid was away. It was so lovely to come home and see her running to greet me as I opened the front door.

She was growing into quite a big cat now. The vet described her as a 'dark torti' and her markings were quite visible. Specks of ginger mingling in her tiny, beige 'bib', matched beigy spots on her front and back paws. She showed enormous affection, and every once in a while, she'd give my cheek a gentle bite - so gentle, it was like a little kiss.

Her cheeky little personality was a joy to watch. She was fascinated by nail polish when she was smaller, and when an Iranian friend came to stay, every time she wriggled her toes, Zoe would pounce on her red varnished toenails—claws and all. She was such fun and I loved her to bits, but poor Mina was terrified of her!

She was my first and only pet, so far. I learned a lot from her and about how we related to each other, and her needs and moods. This opened up a new understanding for me about animals in general, a realization of working and being together on the planet, a new respect for them and their place among us.

I CAN'T REMEMBER EXACTLY HOW long Hamid was away for this time—I think it was about ten months—but his absence made the way clear for God to do a very special type of healing in me of past hurts, which released me more into the freedom He promises to those who follow Him. This was a powerful and life-changing ministry where He took that which held me captive for years in both my mind and emotions, and filled me with new life and a new desire to want to know and follow Him more. The change in me was so great, that it convinced me, once and for all, of the reality and the power of the Living God. His deep healing and determination to 'clean me out' and fill me with His Spirit, anchored me to Him and gave me a new relationship with Him. And because of that, I became part of the healing team at my local church. I had an enormous passion for others to experience God's mighty power to change, to heal, to make lives new, just as I'd experienced.

WHEN HAMID EVENTUALLY CAME BACK, our daily routine changed again, as did our social life, which meant that I wasn't as free to attend church as before. I had taken up piano lessons while he was away and was making good progress. Then, one day, as I was practising my lesson, he walked in and, looking hard at me, said:

You'll have to give this up now. I want to buy a business and I'll need your help in running it.

Stunned by this new decision which, again, he'd made without discussing his plans with me beforehand, I felt that he'd made up his mind, so I just gave up. I hadn't touched a piano since that time (1989) until quite recently (2014).

CHAPTER THIRTEEN

(UNLUCKY FOR SOME…)

It took quite a while to choose the right business. Hamid waded through masses of information about various businesses, and spent more time talking over the phone than not. Then after a huge search and a lot of research, he was attracted to a soft furnishings franchise that offered co-ordinated home interiors, aimed at middle-class professionals.

There were sixty-seven franchises operating at this time and we chose to visit five of them in different parts of the country to see how each one functioned and to get an idea of how popular they were. We were very impressed by what we saw. The franchises were very attractive to the eye, and as we discussed the 'ins and outs' of running a franchise, we were made aware that 'business was booming'. Each time we arrived home from one of these visits, we became more enthusiastic about taking on a franchise of our own. Hamid actually asked for my opinion.

The outlets look lovely, I replied.

So we approached the company who sent us enough

information to tempt us to arrange our first meeting with their franchise director in Bradford. On the day, we were warmly welcomed. We chatted informally about the Company, how the franchises operated, and how we could obtain the necessary funding to finance an outlet, then we were given a tour round head office. From that day on, we were convinced that this was the business for us. The only 'but, what if...' was that, if, for whatever reason, the business should fall through, we would lose our house which the bank required as collateral against any loan we might take out with them. I mentioned this to Hamid as we were trying to reach our final decision about going ahead with purchasing a franchise, but he chose to ignore my doubts. Instead, he contacted head office to arrange an appointment at their bank in Bradford. He'd made up his mind.

DURING THIS TIME, I HAD BEEN suffering considerable pain under my right rib-cage, and after a visit to the hospital, I was scheduled to have surgery to remove my gall-bladder the following month (January, '89). So the franchise was put on 'hold' until after my surgery, which also gave us a bit more time to mull things over.

January came round very quickly, and on that cold and frosty morn, I was wheeled into theatre and surgery began. It went well, and, afterwards, I made good and rapid progress in my recovery, so much so, that I was able to go home within three days.

But it wasn't long before I was back in hospital again, this time fighting for my life. The griping pain in my right lung was getting worse. I couldn't sit, lie down or stand. My GP visited me at home: he took one look at me and asked to use the phone. He came hurrying back saying he had just phoned A&E at the QMC to prepare an emergency room for me. He told us there was no time to wait for an ambulance, that Hamid should drive me there and that he (the doctor) would meet us at the hospital.

Once there, I was whisked away on a trolley and pushed at great speed into a small room. Half a dozen people were running round me, hooking me up to drips and injecting me; the intense activity and the pain were gathering momentum. I realized my life was in danger and I started to panic. Scared and unprepared for death, I started to pray loudly in tongues-—to call on God. The doctors worked faster, hooking me up to the drip that fed Heparin into my bloodstream to dissolve the clot, while Hamid looked on.

You're panicking, someone said. *Try taking deep breaths.*

I tried, but the pain was so bad and I was so scared. I was also aware something else was happening to me: my body was rapidly sinking into the mattress, I was losing control…

I have no idea how long I was sedated for, but I do remember regaining a very woozy consciousness and seeing Hamid sitting in a wheelchair, in a nightshirt, in front of me. When I was able to form a few words I asked him why he was in a wheelchair.

I was taken ill with a high temperature after you were sedated, he said, *so a doctor checked me over and found I had an ingrowing something-or-other and decided I needed immediate surgery!*

I was stunned. We tried to laugh but it was more from disbelief than anything else. We chatted, but sleep quickly began drawing me back again and I lost consciousness once more.

The next time I came round was in the quiet of the night. I lay for a minute or two in the dark trying to remember where I was. There was no one there. I started panicking. I tried to get out of bed but was hampered by drips and tubes fixed to metal stands nearby. I saw a button on the bedside table and pressed it. A young, smiling, Asian man swiftly entered the room.

How are you feeling? He asked kindly, his voice reassuring me that I was safe in his care.

Oh, a bit fuzzy-headed, I replied.

He smiled and asked if he could make me a cup of tea. He stayed with me as I drank it, chatting about this and that, trying to assess whether or not my brain was functioning normally during our conversation.

What are you interested in? He asked.

Music, I love music, came the immediate response.

What kind?

Oh, classical, jazz, bossa nova and good pop.

Do you like Tina Turner?

I love Tina Turner!

I've got my Walkman in my desk, would you like to listen to some music?

Yes I would, thank you.

He quickly returned with the radio and gently placed the headphones over my ears, but they kept slipping down over the back of my head.

It might be better if you sat upright in the chair, he said.

Taking my arm he steadied me as I got down from the bed, and after wrapping a blanket around my shoulders, he placed the headphones on my ears again.

That's better, he said.

Then, fiddling with the buttons on the Walkman, he said:

Press this one to start it, and the other one, underneath, to rewind it. He then left the room saying he would pop in again soon to see how I was doing.

I followed his instructions and the music rushed fast and loud into my senses. The heartbeat of life was in the rhythm and I began weeping at the realization of having been so close to death. I was grateful to God for bringing me back, and, of course, I was so grateful to the staff at the QMC! Now, if ever I mention this period of my life, my voice always quivers as I tell folk that the staff at the QMC saved my life.

The following day, I woke up to find three doctors at the foot of the bed, and Hamid sitting in a chair next to them.

How are you feeling now? asked one.

Much better than when I first came here, I replied.

His female colleague smiled. He continued:

And the pain, how's that?

Much, much less than it was.

Good. The X-ray showed you've had a pulmonary embolism—a travelling blood clot—in your right lung. These things happen sometimes after surgery, even though we administered Heparin at the time.

My first thought was to joke about it.

My family used to say I was a clot!

I smiled and so did the female doctor; but the other two - and Hamid - appeared shocked by what I said. But I think I meant it more to deflect the seriousness of the situation and to help me cope.

Within a few days I was allowed home and left the hospital with a box of anticoagulants and feelings of immense gratitude to the staff who had 'pulled out all the stops' to save my life. I would need to go back as an out-patient shortly, but for the moment, I could settle back in the familiar surroundings of my home.

The cat was as bewildered as we were at the turn of events over the last few days. She was whisked off to my sister's during our time in hospital, and promptly returned when Hamid was discharged. I'd lost track of time and seemed uninterested in knowing just how long I'd been out of action, but I do know that I was very glad to be 'over the worst'.

MY WEAK STATE OF HEALTH WAS VERY obvious over the next few weeks. I was unable to do very much and when I tried, I became incredibly tired and had to rest, so it was obviously going to take a while for me to recover fully. But after a couple of weeks, Hamid started talking again about going ahead with the franchise.

I've been in touch with Carol, he said, *and she suggested another meeting with her and then with the bank to finalise everything and take on the loan. I told her that we'd both been in hospital. She sends you her regards and hopes that you'll be feeling much better soon. The date she proposes for the meeting is the 6th March. In your present state of health, I suggest that you stay home while I go and deal with this myself.*

But I insisted on going, whatever state I was in, as this was a very important step for us, and one, we discovered later, that would affect our lives dramatically, bringing with it changes I hadn't expected.

CHAPTER FOURTEEN

CO-ORDINATED DREAMS

The good thing about taking on the franchise was that there was a 'template' for us to follow, which helped considerably. During the next three weeks Hamid was busy familiarising himself with how our franchise was expected to perform; about how to reach expected sales targets, and what clients could expect from our business. I, on the other hand, was still recovering from my time in hospital. Progress here was slow, and I was still very weak when the shop-fitters moved in to our outlet in the Market Square to fit out the shop. I wanted to be there to see what was happening and how things were taking shape: and in a very short time the business was ready to roll. The buzz of activity had created a lot of interest in passers-by. Some had already popped their heads through the door wanting to know when we would be open for business. In fact, the very last week while the fitters were still working on the finishing touches, people just started walking in and looking around and saying what a lovely shop it was to come into.

Our shop window

...and lovely showroom

When all the work was completed, we waived goodbye to the carpet fitter, the electricians, the display co-ordinators and the window dresser, and we were left standing in the middle of our beautiful showroom, 'holding the baby'. We felt excited but a bit nervous. This was our very first business, and it was gorgeous, but now it was down to us to make it succeed.

The official opening was scheduled for the following Monday, and offers of discounts on curtains, carpets and sofas to entice customers were displayed in the shop. We contacted a local newspaper and asked them to write an article to advertise the business, and on the first day of trading, as the reporter jotted down his impressions, the sparkling wine flowed. It was a really happy time for us - and quite busy! Loads of people came through the door, admiring the décor, chatting and looking through sample books to see what types of styles and fabrics we were offering. We could see from their expressions that they really liked what they saw, and at the end of that hectic first day, we knew we were on to a winner.

So business began well and as the days went by we found that the work wasn't difficult, but, sometimes, the ordering process was, depending on whether things were in stock or not. The hours were long, and some days we wouldn't arrive home until 10 or 11pm. Working six days a week and long hours is possible in the short-term, but the business quickly took over our lives and there was little time for anything else.

One day, a young woman came into the shop and began looking through the fabric samples. She turned to me and started talking. She seemed a nice person and had a great sense of humour which, she added, she'd inherited from her grandfather who was Irish. As we chatted she told me she was actually looking for a job, that she had experience in selling and would love to work in our lovely showroom. She seemed to be one of those special people with a winning personality, and by the time she left that day, I had taken on Jenny O'Hare as a part-time assistant. She proved to be very good with customers and people liked her, she also made life a bit easier for us by taking some of the work off our shoulders.

People kept popping in from the Bradford office to make sure we were OK, and sometimes gave us a hand, and orders were coming in thick and fast, which was a great encouragement. Home appointments where customers chose their colour schemes and fabrics in their home environment were done in the evenings which made the day quite long, usually. Hamid measured and fitted the curtains initially, but eventually, we called on a local fitter to do that.

Things were going well, and nothing seemed too much trouble for head office. Systems within the company proved reliable, and sales built up over the first three months so that by July, we had over £14,000 worth of orders on our books - and what's more, it was summer!

THE EARLY MORNING JULY SUN warmed my back as I unlocked the

shop door one morning. I checked the window before going in to see that everything was in place. The summer sun highlighted the large patterned, soft-green and silver folds of fabric hanging side by side, with their contrasting swags and fancy tie-backs. A small, circular table stood to the left, draped in mosaic-patterned fabric and sumptuously gathered round the bottom, with narrow swags festooned round the top's edge in a plain, contrasting-colour. A large square of soft-green carpet framed in white wood, sat slightly tilting up at the back, in front of the curtains, and to the right of the curtains, stood a three-foot high porcelain plant-stand supporting a bulbous-shaped pot, holding a large, green-leafed, variegated plant. Over in the right corner, a five-foot length of a darker coloured carpet hung vertically from the ceiling behind a large photograph showing a sofa in a coordinated fabric, bringing balance to the whole idea and creating an image of a dream interior. It looked lovely.

The day started just like any other we had experienced there so far, and as I entered the shop, the list of 'things to do' was buzzing round in my head. We had been trading for almost four months now and were feeling more confident about what we were doing. By 10.30am customers were trickling through the door and Hamid and I were busy helping them with their queries. The fax machine was also busy, but so were we, and Hamid didn't pick up the messages till around lunchtime. There was quite a pile by this time. I was still chatting to a customer when he grabbed the faxes and started reading through them.

(1) *Customer's delivery date.* (2) *Fabric out of stock,* he said quietly to himself, flicking the page over. His pace rapidly began slowing down as he quietly concentrated on the next fax, he then left the showroom and disappeared upstairs for a while. When he returned, my customer had left and I was tidying up the sample books. He was at the fax machine hurriedly trying to feed the paper through. I went over to him, he seemed agitated. He looked up at me:

The Company's bank has called in the Receivers. All production, supplies and deliveries have been suspended for the time being.

What?!!

We were both in a state of shock. At the same time, customers were coming into the showroom so there was nothing for it but to carry on doing the job, at least until the end of the day. The fax machine was madly churning out endless documents by now, mostly from other franchisees who were equally shocked by the news and who were also about to lose a lot of money. They were speculating all manner of things and soon established 'round robin' updates to keep everyone informed of the latest events, but each update seemed more dreadful than the previous one.

Why didn't we see it coming, we asked ourselves. We had thoroughly researched the whole thing and hadn't seen anything wrong with it at all. All the figures added up in the Company information we were given prior to purchasing the franchise, so what went wrong?

It was only a matter of days before letters demanding payments that had not been made started arriving. The first was a demand for the previous quarter's rent for the outlet which was £8,000, which we'd already paid to H.O., who held the lease. We forwarded the money weeks before, which they obviously hadn't paid to the landlord, and now we were being threatened with eviction by the landlord who was demanding the money by return post.

Following this, during the next few days, we noticed a man in a black, open-top car parked outside the shop at different times. Then, on another occasion, a very smartly-dressed man came into the showroom asking to see Hamid, who was out at the time. He said he would return later that day, and when he did, it turned out that he was the landlord. Hamid showed him the receipts from H.O., for the £8,000 we had paid them for the rent, to which the landlord said he understood our situation and offered his apologies for being so abrupt with us. But he also said he had a multimillion pound investment in the building to protect and couldn't afford to wait much longer. He left after agreeing to contact H.O., and deal with them directly. Both he, and the man in the car, never bothered us again.

Other demand letters started arriving for the electricity bill, water bill, fabric and accessories bills, which had all been paid by us to H.O., but who, obviously, had not paid the suppliers. It was a nightmare trying to sort out these triangular problems, as the

Receivers were less than co-operative and who now controlled the Company.

We continued trading from the shop as long as we could, but more to keep on top of the problems. A management buyout of the Company was suggested by a small group of franchisees, but after a couple of meetings with the Receivers, they backed off. We still had £14,000 worth of orders on our books to complete so were working extremely hard trying to find alternative solutions and suppliers.

When we attended a creditors meeting in Bradford, the large room was already packed with both angry suppliers and franchisees when we arrived. The directors of the Company apologised, one after another, as they explained how they had taken several 'wrong turns' that led to the Company's downfall.

Our solicitor accompanied us to this meeting and later told us that, having seen the figures, it was unlikely that we would be able to retrieve any money back from the Company as we were way down the list of creditors.

The stress was unbelievable. Friends and family were concerned about what would happen finally, knowing now that our small house was at stake. As the days passed, news came through that the Receivers had agreed to release certain supplies to franchisees, in particular, the Company's own fabrics, which were unique. This was great news for us, because several of our customers' orders were for items in these fabrics. The deal with the Receivers was that when we placed an order with them, we would also send a cheque for the full amount. This we readily agreed to, and the cogs began turning again. We had also managed to find local people to make up curtains for our customers, and this worked very well where we needed fabrics that were more generally available. Our biggest problem was trying to fulfil orders for furniture. The person responsible for supplying furniture, particularly in the Company's own fabrics, left the Company when the Receivers took over. It was such a headache trying to pacify customers and also trying to find out where this man had disappeared to. We wanted him to make up the furniture for us because he knew exactly what we wanted. We found him, eventually, but it took a while.

Some customers were afraid of losing their deposits so they cancelled their orders. It was easier for us to give back their deposits than to run around like headless chickens trying to get their orders processed. But lots of people trusted us to do what we said we'd do, and weren't too bothered about the time it took, once we made them aware of the situation. A couple living in Beeston waited six months for their sofa and never once mentioned cancelling their order. We delivered it to them around 10pm the same day we collected it from Bradford. They were so delighted with it that they made us stay for coffee! We couldn't thank them enough for being so patient and so kind to us at such a difficult time. They were very sympathetic towards us and the problems we were now experiencing. When we left, they asked us to keep in touch with them, but we never contacted them again because we were so involved with sorting out the many complications arising, daily, from what now had become a 'can of worms'.

Our Franchise Agreement stated that the Company would support us through the first year of trading to ensure our success! Huh!!

Another soft-furnishings company came on the scene offering to buy the Company, which it did, including its debts at 25p per pound sterling. They seemed very friendly at first, treating us all respectfully and offering to help us get back on track again. It sounded good initially, until they began listing their terms and conditions, which, when boiled down, amounted to no more than them taking over our franchise and asking us to manage it. In desperation we considered it, briefly, but realized we would still lose the money we'd paid for the franchise, lose our home, and incur a large debt because of the loss of the franchise, so we gave them an emphatic *No, thank you.*

Next came a letter from their solicitor listing our debts to the Company--about £9,000 in all—accompanied by a demand for payment. Worried, we immediately took the documents to our solicitor who chuckled to himself as he read through them, saying:

Don't worry at all about this. They are using the Company's name and logo, so I'll just send them a counter-claim for everything the Company owes you - which is far more than you owe them - that'll shut them up!

And, you know, it did. Not another peep from them. I

was astonished.

But other problems continued. The bank obviously knew what was happening and was keeping a close eye on our 'progress'. We also found that we were experiencing new difficulties now with other suppliers who were aware of our struggling business. Again, we negotiated paying upfront when placing an order with them, to which they agreed. But this, again, affected our customers' confidence in our ability to complete their orders on time, so more deposits were returned. I must say that it was worth returning the deposits just to see the look of amazement on peoples' faces - they were dumbstruck most times! They clearly hadn't expected to get their money back without a tussle, but I knew that God honours honest dealings; they, possibly, didn't. Because of this, people softened towards us, and said kind things like, they hoped things would work out for us.

But 'things' didn't go well. One morning at the shop we opened a letter from the landlord's solicitor informing us that he had been unsuccessful in obtaining the rent from the Company, and that he would issue a notice of eviction from the premises unless we could come up with a further £8,000 for the last quarter, by return post.

Our solicitor had advised us that this would eventually happen, but we still weren't prepared for leaving. We decided to act immediately by closing the shop and turning down the lights, then we began systematically dismantling everything. A friend knocked on the glass door, we let him in and told him what was happening; he asked if he could help. We had no idea he was coming, or that he had his van parked outside! What a God-send he was at this time. We worked long into the night, but, between us, sorted everything out. Various people offered to store things for us the following day, but for now, all we wanted to do was go home and get some sleep.

FABRIC SAMPLES AND SAMPLE BOOKS, display stands, chip-boards, lampshades, carpet, carpet samples, wallpaper sample books, curtain rods, boxes of brass tie-back hooks, boxes of curtain hooks, office furniture and files—all from the shop—filled our home.

After the last item was brought in from the van we closed the front door and shut out the rest of the world. This was a very sad and scary time for us. We had started the business with such joy and expectation. Now, after only a few months, the dream was in tatters.

The cat weaved her way in and out, over and around the piled boxes and fabrics, poking her shiny, little nose into everything as we prepared dinner that night. Our thoughts dominated the silence while going through the practical motions of preparing the food. When it was cooked, we ate it without thinking too much about what we were eating. Afterwards we sat, eyes glazed in front of the television, feeling tired and trying not to think too far ahead.

That night we slept like babes - gratefully drifting off to

where no demands were being made on us. The next day we handed the shop's keys over to the landlord.

THE DAY WAS VERY BUSY INDEED. It started with a phone call to our solicitor who informed us about what we could expect from now on. He explained that the bank would soon start making demands for the repayment of the £36,000 loan we had with them, so Hamid made an appointment to see him.

We sat in his office that morning listening quietly as he instructed us about the action we needed to take.

As far as the bank is concerned, he said, *if you are unable to repay the loan they will take you property. Legally, it's quite straight forward and they'll win. But...* (we were glad to hear this '*but*') *because the bank appears to have had an arrangement with the Company to provide loans to suitable franchisees, we can put in a counter-claim because the bank, it seems, was working with the Company who then recommended it to franchisees as part of the franchise set-up.* He continued: *If you decide to go ahead with this we can finance it through the Legal Aid system as this will be seen as an important case. If we can prove what the bank's position was when the loan was offered, it will set a precedent for the other franchisees (sixty-eight of them) who have taken out loans in this way.*

A ray of hope! We readily agreed to go ahead with the counter-claim. As the week went by we waited for a letter from the bank demanding payment, and sure enough, it arrived. We promptly despatched it to our solicitor who immediately sprang into action, launching a case that lasted four years.

Our solicitor was a clever young man, a keen Christian, and extremely kind to us throughout the duration of our case. He worked very hard to help us and attended every meeting we had with the Company administrators, Uncle Tom Cobley and all.

In-between-time, we were still trying to complete orders from home. We relied heavily on a local curtain maker who came up with the goods every time, meeting every deadline we gave her. What a God-send she was! We were still chasing the Company's exclusive fabrics from other outlets that were still functioning, which sometimes meant travelling long distances to collect. If we experienced further hold-ups from suppliers, we had to deal with some unhappy customers—unhappy more, I think, because they were unsure about whether we could fulfil their orders, which was understandable. Some were also quite nasty.

As time went on, our legal case was hotting up to the point where our solicitor thought it best to employ a barrister from Lincoln's Inn, London, to fight our case at the high court. So we all drove off to London to meet this man.

We sat in his office facing him. He was a handsome man, about thirty-fivish, with jet-black, jelled hair, and when he spoke, he exuded power and authority.

Would you like to choose another solicitor? he asked forcefully.

I couldn't believe what I was hearing; our solicitor was sitting right there in the room with us!

Er, no, we replied, totally unprepared for this question.

So you're happy for Mr. Smith to continue representing you?

Yes.

When he first spoke, his powerful manner just about blew me off my chair! It was hard to imagine him as a man with a soft heart. He must have noticed my reaction, and smiled, relaxing a little, and asked if we'd like a cup of tea.

By the time the tea arrived we had covered most of what we needed to know about how the case would proceed from then on. He turned to our solicitor, chatted with him briefly, then ended on a more humane note saying that he had arranged for us to have lunch at his club. We left his office talking rapidly as we went.

The meal was a very basic liver and onions with mashed potatoes, and not very tasty at that, but at least it kept hunger at bay. Over coffee we discussed the legal path we would take now that the new barrister was in charge of the case. We then headed home feeling much more confident about winning our case than when we'd started out that day.

But that didn't last long. A letter from the bank arrived one day in November telling us it was going to repossess our home. Our solicitor told us to leave it with him, which we did, but a few days later, he contacted us to tell us that this was definitely going to happen and that we needed to find somewhere else to live.

I've asked them to wait until after Christmas, he said, *and they've agreed. The date of eviction will be early next February.*

Our hearts sank at the news. We were working so hard

trying to continue the curtain side of the business from home. We'd managed to organise fabric supplies through another supplier and our local curtain maker was still making up curtains for us. But we were also experiencing a cash-flow problem by this time and tried to get a small loan from our bank, but they refused to lend us any money. We'd been living on our credit cards since we closed the shop and had just about reached our limit.

CHAPTER FIFTEEN

BREAKING UP IS SO VERY HARD TO DO

I have no recollection of what that Christmas was like, except that a very dark cloud hung over us, and soon after, we began sorting and packing our belongings. My sisters and our friends took most of our stuff and stored it for us, and Marj knew someone who let us rent her home for a very modest sum while she worked abroad.

I was busy upstairs sorting things out, one day, when there was a very distinct knock at the door: a knock...knock that reminded me of the bearer of bad tidings in a Dickensian story. I ignored it, for some reason, and carried on working, and when I came downstairs, found a letter lying on the carpet. I picked it up and opened it; it was the anticipated letter of eviction - time and date.

This is it, I said out loud, and threw up a prayer for help.

WE CLOSED THE DOOR OF OUR LITTLE house for the last time on February 9, 1990. Then with cat in carrier, we climbed into the car and drove off to our new home, an old terraced house, not too far away.

Our first surprise was to find another couple living there, which meant we'd have to share the bathroom and kitchen. There were two reception rooms downstairs so we were able to have our own sitting room. There was a small garden at the back for the cat to wander in and she, at least, seemed to take the move in her stride. She was a great comfort during those days; I was so glad to have her with us.

We decided to give up the business altogether at this point and try to find employment elsewhere. I managed to find a part-time job as a receptionist quite easily soon after we moved, but Hamid had more difficulty: it was 1990 and there was a big dip in employment. Right from the beginning, out of choice, Hamid didn't want to apply for British citizenship, and was content with his residential status, but I think this might have gone against him when applying for jobs, despite his good qualifications. His search continued for a further few weeks, by which time, money was in very short supply. So he decided to sign up with an employment agency and took on temporary manual work at different places, ending up on a production line in a factory for several months. The work was repetitious and monotonous and he found the factory floor mentality difficult to deal with, although there were one or two people who were OK. The pay was minimal, but it kept the wolf from the door at that time of need. I admired him very much for taking that decision, considering his background.

I also found my job dull—sometimes working at the reception desk, other times doing low-level admin tasks in the office. There was a bitchy core of females there, always ready with their daily dose of negativity, always ready to pull-down and belittle people. It made me quite nervous - I hadn't thought about having to put up with this sort of thing when I applied for the job. But I know God uses these everyday situations to bring to the surface that in *us* that needs changing. He also wants us to pray for those who upset us because, they too, need the light and love of God in their lives and to be reconnected to the Creator. Many people have very difficult problems in life and I have discovered that God is the first point of call to working things out.

I HAD A LOT OF GOOD AND VARIED work experience, but still felt inadequate because of not possessing any formal qualifications, and this damaged my confidence. I decided to give up my job and take a secretarial course at a local college to gain a few 'strings to my bow', and to become 'computer literate'. Hamid wasn't too pleased about this, but my argument was that, if I were better qualified, I'd be able to get a better job. Reluctantly, he agreed, and I promptly applied for a place on a course. The year went very well indeed, and the course proved to be the right decision. But while I was at the college, I kept noticing adverts for ACCESS courses– ACCESS to university. I started finding out about the course subjects, and my interest grew. I spoke to a tutor who said that if I passed my secretarial course with good grades – including GCSE 'O' level English and Maths, I'd be accepted on the Media and Communication Studies Course. I was so thrilled about the opportunity of a chance to go to university through this course that I was bursting to tell Hamid.

When I got home, he was sitting quietly reading, with the cat sleeping next to him on the sofa.

Hello.

No answer.

Have you had a good day? I persisted.

No answer.

I was quite used to this lack of response. In fact, he seemed to prefer not talking to me, although he chatted and laughed quite freely with others. His sullen behaviour really upset me—he knew that—and that, it seems, is what he liked to do. He often went out in the evenings and weekends on his own, never saying where he was going. Some time went by before I discovered he was attending TM sessions, and also a Sufi group he'd found not far away. He also went to the cinema, attended lectures, and was getting involved in academic discussions. None of these activities included me, not even by shared discussion, although, I wouldn't have been interested in TM or Sufism. Something was happening to his mind where he was separating himself from me even more. I felt completely helpless as I failed to 'reach' him. He was alienating himself so much that I became concerned about his mental health.

One day, during this time, he came home from work; I was in the kitchen cooking dinner. I went over to kiss him and say hello, when suddenly, he said:

Do you want me to hit you?

I was so shocked by this strange response that I became angry and told him that if he hit me, I would hit him back! He never did hit me, but this definite change of behaviour was for the worse.

I TOOK A DEEP BREATH AND began talking about college, gathering momentum as I steered my thoughts in the direction of the ACCESS course. I jumped in with both feet.

There's something called an ACCESS course which, if you pass, enables you to take a degree course at university. I spoke to one of the tutors today who explained the course content and said that, because I'd been a partner in a business, and, providing this year's exam results met the criteria, he would give me a place on next year's course.

His angry response was immediate.

And who do you think is going to fund this course?

Oh, the tutor said I might be able to get a grant. It's a great opportunity, I enthused, *one I thought I'd never have.*

Well, you'd better forget about that, he said. *I can't stand life here anymore, I want us to go back and live in Iran where we have our own home and where I'd be able to get a decent job.*

Now I can see that, for him, things would work out well in

Iran, but for me, I would disappear into nothingness again.

Moving back must have been what he'd been contemplating and refused to talk about until now.

I suddenly went mad, shouting at the top of my voice. He started talking about the mess we'd got ourselves into.

WE? I yelled. *Didn't I point out to you when we were talking about taking on the franchise that we could lose our home if the business went through? But you just ignored that completely and went ahead with it!*

This was the first time I'd openly criticized his decision; I'd held back because I knew he felt bad enough about it without me saying (screaming!) anything.

I've made up my mind and I won't change it, he said. *I'm going whether you come or not.*

I started yelling again, this time with tears streaming down my face.

After all we've been through together, not just here, but in Iran, too. How can you just toss me aside like that?

I've made my decision, he said, *and that's that. There are no prospects for me here. You can come with me, if you want to.* And with that, he got up and walked out of the house - his way of dealing with conflict.

How much can a person cry? My worst fear had come upon me. He was leaving me after twenty three years of marriage.

I felt very strongly that returning to Iran was a retrograde step. I felt it so strongly from that time to the present day that I think it came from God. I had no good feeling at all about returning to Iran, only feelings of foreboding. Iran is no ordinary place. I knew it was a wrong step, and I decided to stay in Britain. But how can a person live with a broken heart?

He waited another four months before leaving, and when the day came, I drove him to the coach station. We unloaded his luggage from the car together as the coach pulled in. There was little time for an emotional parting, although, having said goodbye so many times over the years, this seemed like one of those times. We tried to remain unaffected, and smiled.

Have you got everything? I asked, awkwardly.

Think so, he replied.

I handed him a card–it was his birthday the following day.

Save it till tomorrow.

He took it saying he'd better get on the coach. This time there was no hug, no kiss goodbye. We both knew, now, that something different was happening.

Write soon and let me know how things are, I shouted as he boarded the coach. He sat by a window near the front; I waited for him to look over to me and wave, but he didn't. He busied himself with sorting out his bags then chatted to the passenger in the next seat. I stood watching, silently, until the coach crawled out of the bay onto the exit lane and out of the station. That was the last time I saw my husband.

I WAS 'TEMPING' DURING THE SUMMER holidays at the University,

The last photo I took of Hamid before we separated

and when I arrived for work the following day, my colleagues already knew what had happened the day before and were sympathetic. A couple of days later, I developed a pain in my right side near my bottom rib. It became so bad that I told my supervisor, saying that I was afraid it might be another embolism. She immediately dropped whatever she was doing, grabbed her car keys - and me - and, at top speed, rushed me over to the hospital, where I spent the next few days. The doctor did all the tests and found that I didn't have an embolism this time - thank goodness - but admitted he didn't know why I had this particular pain. I was given pain-killers and told to rest. This I did, and was able to return to work in due course.

CHAPTER SIXTEEN

WHEN THINGS GET TOUGHER

September 1993 was the beginning of a new era in my life. Soon after Hamid left, my landlady, back from her travels, told me she needed my room so that her elderly mother could come and live with her, so I should find somewhere else to live. I rang a friend who offered me a temporary stay, but soon after I moved on to more permanent accommodation nearer the college.

Two moves in about two and a half months is no easy thing to do, but the house was in the right place for me—not too far from the college. First, I contacted the landlord who told me he'd just taken over the property and intended to rent out the six rooms separately, and that the kitchen and bathrooms would be shared. I arranged a time to see the place and, because I was at the front of the queue, was given first choice. I moved in the next day.

My stark, brilliant-white room must have been the master bedroom on the first floor of a large, 1920/30, two storey, semi-detached house. A wall of cream-coloured, built-in wardrobes and cupboards, edged and embellished by a thin, embossed, gold, leafy pattern, were arranged around the central, rectangular mirror fixed horizontally to the wall above a built-in dressing table. I felt relieved to know there was plenty of cupboard space to put all my stuff in! The room was big enough to fit a three-seater sofa near the back wall; a double-bed over the other side of the room; a small fridge in the corner; my desk and computer, and a small table and chair in front of the tall window. From the window, just below sill level, I could see the changing colours of autumn tree tops along the dappled street.

There were two other unoccupied rooms on this floor, and a largish, shared bathroom. Later, as other tenants began living there, I was surprised to find that the bathroom was kept remarkably tidy, most of the time. But not so the kitchen! This large, rectangular room was divided into two halves by a long row of mahogany base units, with a fitted kitchen over one side of the room, and a carpeted dining area over the other. A smaller bathroom (which had been added more recently) led off from the kitchen, and opposite the mahogany base units, the back door opened out onto a small, lawned garden.

Sharing a kitchen with a lot of very different people who are not family is testing, especially when not all the tenants get along with each other. The house phone was situated in the dining area so there was very little privacy for those using it. Often, messages weren't passed on to others who weren't in to take their calls, and this built up bad feelings between folk who, really, just wanted their own space. We were a mix of both older students and working people. No-one was below the age of twenty-three, and I was the eldest among them.

The college was just three bus-stops away, and a nice walk on a nice day. For me, the course wasn't easy; I hadn't done any academic study for years, and was frightened of failing. My self-esteem was at zero level especially after splitting up with Hamid. I felt very nervous when having to answer questions in class or give a presentation. I had no idea how to present myself or my work in a positive light, or what I was capable of doing. But I was encouraged to 'launch out' and form my own opinions again, which had been discouraged by the men in my life and treated with disdain by both my father and my husband. I grew as a person in that year, and when I left the course, I could see the change in me.

THE FIRST LETTER I RECEIVED FROM HAMID was dated 2 August '93, although it arrived quite a while after that date. The tone was very upbeat and descriptive about his friends meeting him when he arrived at Tehran airport, and how good it was to be back in Iran. He ended the letter saying:

Let me know what's happening regarding housing and your exam results. Look after yourself and please write regularly. Love, Hamid.

I think he said more to me in those three pages than he had done all year!

The next letter was dated 15 August '93.

It is now eighteen days since I arrived in Tehran and I haven't had any letters from you. Hope you are well and getting things sorted. I love you always, Hamid.

I was completely baffled! I hadn't written to him because I felt so angry about him leaving me. He'd shown me in the past that he'd do whatever he wanted, regardless of what I thought. I know for sure he thought I'd follow him, as I had done before, when I 'came to my senses'(!).

I feel sure that this festering attitude began with his mother, who, according to him, used to try to thwart his activities every time he wanted to go climbing or skiing with his friends, before we were married. She was afraid something might happen to him. She didn't realize that, then, he was both a highly skilled climber and a competent skier who could well fend for himself.

When I'd calmed down a bit I decided to phone him. He told me about all the trips he'd made since his return and how perfect the timing had been.

I listened.

I'd only been back a few days, he said, *when I heard that some of our relatives were legally trying to take possession of our apartment.* (Because of the political problems we were unable to sell, so rented it out while we were in Britain.)

So I found out the date of the court hearing and secretly went there. I sat with a crowd of others so the relatives wouldn't see me - they had no idea I was back in Iran. Anyway, when the presiding judge read out my name and asked if I was present, I sprang to my feet and answered with a loud, Yes, I am! The rellies couldn't believe it! They thought it would be a cinch—no contest at all. Well, I showed them. The case finished very abruptly after that!

That was one good thing that happened as a result of him going back. His conversation was quite buoyant as we chatted, but when we said goodbye, I put down the phone and sat for a long time in the quietness feeling so sad that events had driven us apart, yet knowing full-well that the only solution to our situation, as far as Hamid was concerned, was for me to pack up and go to live with him in Iran. I knew in the depth of my heart that I couldn't do that.

The cat was becoming increasingly precious to me now Hamid was no longer here. She seemed to understand when I was upset about something, and was a great comfort when I felt sad. She was also a great joy and helped me stay focussed on the practical things I needed to do each day. When she was ill or went missing for hours on end, I, then, worried about her, instead of my own situation.

THE COLLEGE YEAR WENT BY VERY QUICKLY and I managed to pass the ACCESS course. By this time, most of my classmates were on track for their chosen degree courses at university. I had applied for a place to 'do' psychology at one of our local universities, but was rejected after my interview.

We've never known that happen before, said my tutor. He also said the same thing about the full grant I received when I first started the ACCESS course. But I can now see God's hand was both giving and also guiding me to another university and a very different course which I would start later on in two years' time.

I needed to work so joined an agency again 'temping' in various places. I had to manage my money very carefully during this time, because sometimes I had work and, other times, I didn't. But my sister, Marj and her husband, kept an eye on me and helped me out when I was struggling. Through their help and concern for me, I became aware of the plights of others. It opened my eyes to those needing help and made me think of ways I could help them. This was the beginning of a turning point for me away from always being on the receiving end, which had occurred as a result of all the disastrous events that had happened, so far.

CHRISTMAS DAY ARRIVED SOONER THAN EXPECTED. The date was still the same as it had always been, but the time leading up to it seemed to rush by. I busied myself in the morning trying to wrap presents before heading off to spend the next two days with my sister and the family. Still busy cutting and sticking paper, I heard the phone ring downstairs, so ran down to catch the call before the ringing stopped. It was Sarah, the sister of a girl whose room was on the ground floor.

Hello, Bobbi, Merry Christmas! She chirped, then continued: *Is Debbie there, please?*

I went and knocked on Debbie's door, but there was no

answer. I knocked louder, calling to her saying that her sister was on the phone, but there was no reply, so I went back to tell Sarah.

That's funny, she said, *she's supposed to be here - now! Do you know if she's already left the flat?*

I don't, I replied: *but if you hang on, I'll take a look outside to see if her car's there.* I nipped to the front door and saw her car was still outside, so came back and told her.

I wonder where she is then, although, she could still be asleep - she's a pretty heavy sleeper. O.K, don't worry, I'll phone her later.

I ran back upstairs, finished wrapping the presents, grabbed my coat and keys and hurried downstairs to my car. It was almost 1pm and I should have been sitting down for Christmas lunch now, but still had half an hour's travel ahead of me.

Marj and Dave had also invited a couple of friends to stay whom I knew well, and for the next two days we all made ourselves 'at home' enjoying their wonderful hospitality and a lovely, family Christmas. But the time passed by all too quickly, and after saying our goodbyes on Boxing Day, I returned home that evening, laden with gifts.

I was just about to put the key in the lock when my next door neighbour and his wife called me over. They were both dressed in white, towelling, dressing-gowns, and slippers.

Come in, Bobbi. We're just about to make a drink - would you like something? they asked.

Oh, no thanks, I replied.

They both looked at me seriously, then Richard

began saying:

We're sorry to have to tell you but we've got some bad news. The police were called to your house on Christmas day by Debbie's sister who had been trying to contact her, but couldn't. They came and broke down the door and found her dead in bed - she'd had a massive heart attack. An ambulance came, and we eventually saw the men carry a body to the ambulance in a black bag.

I was stunned.

But she was only in her thirties, I managed to say.

I know, they said, sadly.

She was so fit, she was in the T.A. What caused it? I asked.

We don't know, they mumbled. *Are you sure you wouldn't like a drink?*

No thanks, I replied. *I'd better get home and phone my sister to tell her what's happened. What a shock - and at Christmastime, too. It's such a bad time for those left behind. Christmas will never be the same again for them.*

I felt both sad and confused as I went home. I left them standing on the doorstep waiting to see me safely inside the house. Most of the other tenants were still away for Christmas so the house seemed a bit spooky after being told the news about Debbie. The transience of life, and a life cut short were thoughts uppermost in my mind now, at this, usually, joyful time of year.

CHAPTER SEVENTEEN

OH, MUM!

I returned to work in the new year at the company that supplied books to libraries and academic institutions, where I had been temping since before Christmas. I was employed as a receptionist/personnel assistant, and one day, the personnel officer came to me and said that the company was advertising this job and asked if I'd be interested in applying for it.

It's not the sort of job I'm looking for, I replied. *I'd like a job where I can use my head a bit more...and the pay is quite low, I need to earn enough to live on long-term.*

Well, it is permanent and you'd have a regular salary coming in every month, so think about it.

I watched her small, navy suited body turn and walk away, her black, curly, shoulder-length hair bobbing up and down as she went. She was a nice lady, not too clever, but nice. I went home and thought about what she'd said. The words 'regular income, permanent job' finally persuaded me to take up her offer. It was what I needed to get me through the next few months, and it would help me keep a roof over my head and pay off a few small debts.

IT WAS DURING THIS TIME THAT my mother kept falling down. The first time it happened, she fell all her length while crossing a road. After a few more falls she decided to consult her doctor and was later diagnosed with motor neurone disease.

Mum was a smallish, plump lady. She'd always been extremely active throughout her life. She still lived at home and wanted to continue to, so my sisters and I regularly popped in to see her. But as the disease progressed, and after she'd had yet another fall, we decided to ask her GP to re-assess her. She told us that mum's condition was deteriorating very quickly now, and that we should consider getting her into a residential care home, because we wouldn't be able to cope as the illness worsened. So my sister and her husband promptly began seeking a suitable residential home in the area and finally chose a newly built care home not too far from where we all lived, so that we could visit mum regularly.

Mum wasn't happy about giving up her home and going in to residential care. Like many of her generation, she viewed going in to 'care' with suspicion, and as something to be feared. But we reasoned with her and told her that her GP had advised it, so she agreed to go with us and take a look at her potential new 'home'. She actually liked it! She was impressed by how nice the place was

Mum in the middle between my sisters Marj (to the left) and Pat and Ranzo (the dog) to the right, with Jenny standing behind her next to me

and by the lovely, sunny room she would have, so much so, that she decided to move in. But, sadly, it wasn't too long before matron called us into her office, one day, to tell us that mum's condition was rapidly worsening and that the care home didn't provide nursing care. She advised us to get her into a nursing home, which we did, but she passed away just three weeks later.

The 17th July 1995 was a very sad day indeed. It's hard to lose your mother - even when your relationship with her hasn't been that good. It had been very distressing to see her increasingly frustrated as she tried to do and say things. Her mind had remained sharp, but her body had quickly lost its ability to function. At the crematorium, I stood between my sisters, holding hands with them as we watched her coffin shunt through the barrier that separated us forever.

Contact with Hamid had been less frequent during the months leading up to mum's death, and it was quite a while after that that I wrote to tell him that she had died. He wrote back saying how sorry he was to hear the news, offering his condolences to the rest of the family. I was surprised that he didn't phone, after all the meals she'd cooked and all the sweaters she'd knitted for him, I thought he might. She was, after all, his mother-in-law, and I was—legally—still his wife.

He mentioned in his letter that he was finding it difficult to write to me because my last letter to him had been harsh. (I must have written to him when I was feeling angry with him for leaving me with all the problems I was facing. I needed my husband's support physically, mentally, emotionally and financially.) He said that we should forget the past, heal the wounds and bridge the gaps and ask for God's guidance. He continued:

We've lived a lifetime together and shared many ups-and-downs. We still have a lot more in common than many other couples I know. He ended the letter with, *I do love you and miss you very much. Lots of love, Hamid.*

Of course this letter made me cry. These are fine words when you're far away from the one they're intended for. I was becoming sceptical about these long distance sentiments. His behaviour, for years, had left me in no doubt now that there were many sides to Hamid. I believe that when he wrote these words he was sincere, but I also know that after a while of being in his company again—especially in Iran where I couldn't leave the country without his permission—he would start behaving badly towards me. I also knew in my heart of hearts that without a change of heart from him, there was no hope in trying to live together again. He had left me 'high and dry' with no money, no home, and a long court case that lasted four years. I was left with absolutely nothing, except the clothes I stood up in. How could I ever trust him again to take care of me, to see that I was safe in his country, and treated well? Worst of all had been his cold-heartedness towards me when he was here in Britain; I couldn't bear that again. I'd loved him so much—and he knew it—but he seemed to see love as something out of his control, and, therefore, wasn't prepared to surrender to it. I thought that, at times, he enjoyed being mean and heartless towards me and seeing me upset, which to me, is love's opposite. So now I was thinking about our past experiences with my head, and not my heart's longing for how I'd like our relationship to be. A big shift of change in perspective was becoming apparent.

PEOPLE AT WORK WERE REALLY KIND TO me following mum's demise and it eased the pressure of trying to cope in a normal, working situation whilst still grieving. It was really nice to see that they could be compassionate as well as efficient.

As time went on, colleagues began expressing concern about rumours of redundancies, which, by now, was the main topic of conversation at work. And as the weeks went by, people were being asked to leave the company, one after another. My boss was one of the first to go, then my colleague with whom I shared my job. I thought I might be next in line, but was told that my job was safe. I couldn't trust those words, somehow, but, then again, I don't think I trusted anyone any more. But my job *was* safe, and it was safe for the rest of the time I worked there.

But feelings of uncertainty about my job made me start thinking seriously about applying for a place at university again. So I dug out my best essays from my ACCESS course, found out the name and address of a psychology lecturer at Nottingham Trent University, wrote him a letter saying that I was interested in doing a degree in psychology, posted it all off, then waited to see what sort of response I'd get–not even thinking about what time of year it was. To my astonishment, I received a reply quite quickly, and was given a date for an informal interview with the tutor I had written to.

When I arrived at his office on the day, I was warmly welcomed and asked to sit down. He told me he liked the work I had sent him from my ACCESS course, and asked me a few questions about what I had done work-wise.

Unfortunately, I can't offer you a place on this September's course, simply because there aren't any places left. But if you want to wait till next year, you'll be the first person on the list, he said.

I mumbled something about wanting to start the degree this September.

Then, what I suggest you do is try to get on another course, then switch courses. There shouldn't be any difficulty with that because some students always drop out after the first few weeks.

That sounded like a better idea. He suggested I try getting a place on their Humanities Course, saying that I shouldn't have any difficulty with that as there were two hundred places on it. But when I tried, I was told that all the places were taken. So I rang the University for advice.

It might be better if you write directly to a tutor on the course, the administrator informed me, adding that there were still places on the Communication Studies Programme. So, again, I bundled my essays, along with a letter, into an envelope and posted it off that day. A few weeks went by and family and colleagues kept asking if

I'd heard anything from the tutor.

Not yet, but I'll let you know when I do, I replied.

Time was moving on and it was getting towards the middle of August now and I still hadn't heard anything. I was getting a bit anxious because I had no desire to stay in my job, and my mind was fixed on going to university. I hadn't given 'not going' a second thought! One evening I came home from work and found a large, manilla envelope on the kitchen table addressed to me. I opened it and took out a wad of paper, on top of which was a letter saying:

Dear Mrs. Davari, Congratulations on your success in obtaining a place on the Communication Studies Degree Programme for 1996-1999.

What? I said out loud as I emptied the rest of the envelope's contents, spreading out the course and enrolment information on the table.

But they haven't even seen me, I said out loud again; but then thought that the lecturer I saw previously must have been in touch with someone on the course, because I mentioned that interview in my letter.

I couldn't believe it! I rang my family and friends to tell them I'd been accepted. They seemed pleased for me because I now knew the direction I'd be taking for the next three years.

I FELT A SENSE OF GOING INTO THE EXCITING UNKNOWN when I handed in my resignation at work.

But you're the one we wanted to stay on, I was told.

What they didn't know was what lay ahead of me was an opportunity I thought I'd never have, so there was no going back now.

I worked my notice, finished my job, donned a pair of jeans and picked up my bag with all my kit in it and joined the other new-comers to the course in 'Freshers' Week'. They were mostly eighteen years old - I was forty nine, and by far the oldest student on the course. As the weeks went by, the Communications Programme, which included a psychology module for the duration of the course, grabbed my interest, so I decided to stay on it.

Getting to grips with all the reading was one of my biggest difficulties in the first year. I would take far too many books from the library, hoping to read them all, then felt swamped by too much information. I had to learn to narrow down the reading quite a bit so that I could read up on all my course subjects, which wasn't easy. I later realized this was a common problem students experienced.

During this time I also took on a part-time job in the Careers Advisory office on campus, which gave me a bit of extra money to top up my grant. So, with my course and my job, I didn't have much time to dwell on the unresolved issues in my life, which was a good thing.

I was still living in the same shared accommodation and had asked the landlord if I could move downstairs to the front room which he was now re-letting after Debbie's demise. He agreed, so I moved my furniture downstairs to the ground floor.

The room must have been the lounge and the dining room

when it was a family home. The dividing wall between the two rooms had been removed, creating a very spacious area where I could spread out my furniture. It had a nice, mid-blue, fitted carpet, with a contrasting coloured pattern at regular intervals; and a long, chunky railway sleeper as the mantelpiece above a large, open fireplace which I made good use of during the winter months. I used this half of the room as my sitting room, placing an armchair by the side of the fireplace, opposite the large bay window that looked out on to the road, and the sofa along the back wall, opposite the fire. I divided the room by putting my desk and computer behind the armchair, long-ways to the door, to obscure the view of the other half of the room where I had my bed and wardrobe. The French windows next to the wardrobe opened out on to the back garden which was really quiet early in the mornings, and where, later, I was stung by a dozy, September-wasp among the runner beans that overhung the fence from next door. Tucking a small fridge in an alcove the other side of the window was the last thing to do and once done, I began settling in.

Being on the ground floor meant that I was able to have a bit more privacy. The kitchen, dining room and the shower room were also on the ground floor, and when I cooked a meal, I would take it back to my room to eat in front of a glowing fire in winter, or with a gentle breeze wafting the curtains through the French window in summer.

I made new friends at a new church—St. Paul's,

West Bridgford—who were incredibly kind and welcomed me into their homes. They were clearly interested and concerned to hear about the unusual events in my life. I answered their questions about how I came to be living west of the city, and they were very sympathetic towards the break-up of my marriage. They offered me friendship and moral support which helped hugely at that time.

As the months went by contact with Hamid was becoming sparse. I still felt angry with him and also powerless to change things. These feelings were particularly strong when I began suffering from periods of severe back pain, which lasted about three weeks at a time, when I was incapable of doing anything at all: I was in agony. When I was able to walk, I had to use two walking sticks for support. I was very dependent on my sister's help then. At these times I found Hamid's, seemingly, not wanting to find out how I was, and his lack of concern about how I was managing, particularly hard to take. My recurring thoughts were on why I had bothered to waste all those years with this man for it all to end like this.

It was during this time that one of the tenants sharing the house started being a nuisance. He was a big, surly chap who liked to throw his weight around. Why he picked on me I really don't know.

One day he started an argument and tried intimidating me by standing about four inches away from me, pointing his finger at my face and yelling abuse. But a very interesting thing happened which I now recognise as God's power. I relaxed completely and kept looking straight at him, letting him carry on ranting. I wasn't in the least bit afraid of him and he suddenly became aware of that. The look on his face showed he was really puzzled by this, and he swiftly turned and, still shouting, marched upstairs to his room. To my amazement I charged after him trying to make him understand things from my point of view! He kept stopping and turning towards me, still carrying on the drama, but I was still unafraid. He opened the door of his room and slammed it behind him telling me to *f*** off*!

There were other occasions where I had to call the police to whom he lied about me saying that 'I had it in for him'. I was very hurt by this, because it was completely untrue; I was just defending my property. If anything, I had tried to help him when he was unemployed by encouraging him to take an ACCESS course and go to university, which I felt he was quite capable of doing and which he did, eventually.

It's a very sad thing when men with problems start picking on women because they think they're an easy target. It's also a very sad thing to be lied about, and especially to the police. It removes any hope of justice in a situation.

But this situation didn't last long. When I went to the university that day I spoke to one of my tutors about it, who suggested I left the house immediately. She contacted the campus accommodation service and found me a room on a temporary basis on campus that I could move into that day. I went to see my sister who was working in the university's counselling service at the time, and arranged to meet her so that we could go together to see the room. But before we even arrived there, she said:

I don't want you to have to move there and then move again when you find somewhere more permanent; come and stay with us instead. In fact, let's go and get some of your things so that you can come and stay tonight, then we'll sort out the furniture later on in the week.

I was so surprised by this but also immensely relieved and grateful for an immediate and safe solution to this awful problem. This big change in circumstances happened within an hour of going to see my tutor, and later made me think that when God says it's time to go, it's time to go.

I began settling in at my sister's and started to relax a bit, knowing that I was in a safe place, and having more contact with the rest of their family gave me a sense of family life again. I missed being part of a family.

Although Hamid and I had no children, we had become a family, and even when we were living in Iran, his family took the place of my family. But now, with mum gone, the centre of the family wasn't there anymore and I felt adrift, not knowing where I belonged.

I MANAGED TO SCRAPE through my first year at university but then, the work hadn't been too difficult, in fact it was quite similar to the work I'd done on the ACCESS course, though there were new ways of looking at things to get to grips with. Passing that first year was a big relief after all the difficulties I'd experienced, as well as the upheaval of moving house again.

It was the end of term with long, sunny days ahead to look forward to and warm evenings out on the patio having dinner with the family. One day, during this time the phone rang; it was Sadeqh, an Iranian friend.

Hello Bobbi, how are you? I've had such a job trying to find you. I had to phone the local council to get your brother-in-law's number because I remembered he is a teacher and would be listed with them. I'm afraid I've got some bad news about Hamid: he's had a heart attack and is in the CCU at a hospital in Tehran.

A few seconds passed.

Are you still there?

Yes, I'm still here. When did it happen? My emotions were gathering pace and I started to panic as the news sank in and I began reconnecting to my long-distant husband.

About ten days ago.

How is he now?

He's better than when it first happened, but the doctor said it would take some time before he could do things normally.

We chatted a while and he suggested I got my Iranian passport sorted out to go to visit him. He didn't have a contact number for the hospital, but said that he'd try to get one. I thanked him for going to all that trouble to find me, then slowly placed the phone down on the receiver rest.

BUT YOU CAN'T GO BACK THERE! My sister was trying to reason with me.

I can't ignore him at a time like this, I insisted anxiously, my mind in rescue mode. I could never figure out what it was about Hamid that made me respond in this way, even right from the beginning when I first knew him. I could blindly pack my case, catch a plane, and go with him without thinking about my own safety.

You don't have the money to go, my brother-in-law chipped in.

I'll ask Ken to lend me the money. And with that, I ran upstairs to dig out my documents for my passport. I then rang the passport office at the Iranian Embassy only to be told that there were no details relating to my previous passport on their system.

When did you last visit Iran?

1986, I replied.

And you travelled using an Iranian passport?

Yes.

Well there's no record of that here. We'll have to issue a new passport, so please bring all your supporting documents with you.

How soon will it be ready? I asked apprehensively.

Oh, in a few weeks, he replied.

I'm sorry I can't wait that long. My husband's just had a severe heart attack and I need to go to Iran quickly.

Come and see me tomorrow, he said offering a ray of hope.

I took his name and told him that I would be travelling down to London from Nottingham by coach.

Don't worry, he said, *just ask for me at the desk when you get here and I'll sort out your details.*

I then rang an Iranian friend living in London to ask if she was free to meet me at the Embassy.

Oh course, Bobbi jan (Bobbi, dear) she said.

I was so grateful to her because she'd be able to deal with the situation from an Iranian standpoint. We arranged to meet outside a shop in High Street, Kensington. The Embassy was just round the corner.

Manijeh had been a friend of ours for many years, but because Hamid and I were no longer together, I hadn't contacted her for a long time. She was as good-natured as ever when we met up again, and greeted me with a kiss on both cheeks. She had married a British doctor since moving to the UK after experiencing a terrible heartache in Iran, followed by a painful legal case. It was so awful it's hard to imagine how she managed to cope with the memory of it all.

Before she married she lived with her elderly mother in Tehran. One day she returned home from work to find her mother stabbed to death in the hallway. She later discovered that a drug-addict had broken into the family home looking for money. Her mother had heard a noise and went to see what it was. Discovering the burglar, she challenged him, but he had a knife and attacked her with it, stabbing her several times. Manijeh said that when she found her there was blood everywhere.

Her mother, a widow, was a very kind and gracious lady. Her love for others inspired us all to love her in return. I was horrified to hear the terrible details of how she died, and deeply saddened for Manijeh, but the story didn't end there.

When Manijeh had recovered a little from the initial horror of finding her mother so brutally killed, she became so angry that she set out to try and find the murderer. How she managed to find him I don't know, but find him she did and he was arrested and later taken to court, and when all were assembled, the trial began.

Who has brought this man to court today? asked the judge.

I have, replied Manijeh.

What right do you have to bring this man to trial?

He murdered my mother—he stabbed her to death, she answered.

You (being a woman) are only worth half the value of a man, therefore, you cannot bring any charge against him. If you want to pursue this case, you will have to pay the equivalent value (thousands of tomans) of the worth of a man to give you equal status.

As she told me her story my heart went out to her. I was enraged at the lack of compassion and the cold-heartedness of that judge: if I'd been in her place I'd have gone crazy. But she knew what to expect, she had lived under the new regime for a few years by this time, so, determined to find justice, gathered together a huge amount of money and paid the fee for equal status with the man(!) who had murdered her mother, so that the trial could begin.

The killer was eventually convicted and justice was done there, but the appalling legal attitude towards Manijeh was doubly grievous at such a terrible time. Soon after the case ended she left Iran and came to Britain to live.

Greatly saddened by her terrible ordeal, I found it hard to say any words of comfort as we ate lunch in a little Italian restaurant near the Embassy. Having known and loved her mother I felt very upset about it all for weeks afterwards. I kept thinking of the terrible way she died and the awful injustice Manijeh had experienced at such a time. And this began to influence my thoughts, powerfully, about travelling to Iran.

We set off for the Embassy putting on our head scarves as we went, pulling them down over our hair as we neared the corner of Prince's Gate. Once inside, I explained my situation to the man I had spoken with over the phone, who then told me to take all my documents downstairs to the Passport Section—which I did. I was given a form to fill in and asked to provide two passport-size photographs (which I didn't have) and return all the documents to him when everything was completed. Manijeh helped me fill in the form—it was written in Farsi—then we left the building to go and find a studio where I could have the photographs taken. We found an Iranian photographer who had a studio just round the corner (clever man) who knew exactly how the head scarf should be placed on my head for an official photograph. This was a big help because without this advice, the Embassy could have said that the photographs weren't right. But everything was OK when I later handed over the documents, and after paying the passport fee, I was told that the Embassy would contact me once my passport was ready for collection. Again, I asked how long it would take to process, telling him why I needed to get to Iran quickly.

Leave it with me, I'll get it processed as quickly as I can. He smiled.

I was so grateful to hear that he understood my concern—a thing I hadn't expected from him. I smiled and thanked him and said goodbye.

I'm always deeply touched by another's unexpected understanding and wanting to help in these sort of situations. I didn't expect to encounter compassion and understanding there, and when I did, I was overwhelmed by emotion and wanted to cry. He touched me with his kindness which I'll always remember.

I was full of anxiety as I travelled back home. Manijeh's story about the terrible injustice she had suffered in Iran was uppermost in my mind. I was also disturbed knowing that Hamid was very ill in that country where women were treated so harshly. I was beginning to worry about going into that situation, but at the same time, felt I had to go. I was already beginning to feel the octopus's tentacles wrapping themselves around me, taking me captive.

Dear Manijeh. *Keep in touch, Bobbi jan,* she said kissing me again on both cheeks as we said goodbye, but I've only seen her once since then. Keeping in touch has become something I'm not very good at.

BACK HOME THE NEXT DAY I contacted Ken, another brother-in-law, to ask him to lend me the money for the trip. When I contacted him, he and my sister, Jenny, wanted to come over and talk to me first about going to Iran—or as it turned out—about *not* going.

And what if, for some reason, you can't get out of Iran, what happens then?

Ken was thinking back to the time during the revolution when all flights were cancelled for long periods due to strike action. I knew in my heart that that was a valid question. Hamid could legally keep me there against my will if he wanted to, but foolishly, I chose to ignore that. I argued and tussled over Ken's and others' concerns, till, in my worried state, I burst into tears, at which point he gave up trying to persuade me not to go and handed me a cheque for a thousand pounds.

The following day I rang the university to tell them what had happened and to ask if I could defer my course for a year. The course administrator was very understanding and said that it was possible to do that. I felt a sense of relief as I spoke to her because getting my degree had become very important to me.

So now, having done all that I needed to do, I waited for my passport to arrive. But despite the circumstances, it still took a while to come through.

Meanwhile, I was in touch with Hamid several times a week finding out how he really was, and found that as the days went by, he was improving, slightly. I told him that I was preparing to come over to see him.

You're coming to Iran? He seemed surprised but sounded weak. His tone softened: *I'm so glad, when is your flight?* He sounded relieved.

I haven't booked it yet, I'm still waiting for my passport to arrive.

In the days ahead, I busied myself with buying things to take to Iran and then packing. The cat was to stay with my sister and the family, so I didn't need to worry about her; and everything else seemed to slot into place until the Embassy contacted me and asked me to collect my passport in person.

Can't you post it on to me? I asked.

No, came the reply, *you must travel to London to collect it.*

He paused, then continued:

Oh, by the way, this passport is only a temporary document that allows you to travel one-way to Iran. You must obtain a new passport while you're there to leave the country.

I thanked him and put the phone down; my brain was now in overdrive.

What if you can't get out of Iran, what then? Ken's words kept repeating over and over in my head. I hurriedly went to the kitchen to talk to Dave whose good counsel has helped me on a number of occasions.

I know it's very hard to face the fact that you may not be able to leave Iran once there, but you must face up to that very strong possibility. Do you want to live in Iran in that (political) situation: wouldn't it be better to have the freedom to decide for yourself whether or not you want to stay?

Of course he was right. I tried to think of a way round it, but there wasn't one. That night was a very long, dark night of soul-searching and praying for guidance to make the right decision. By morning I'd decided not to go. I couldn't bear to tell Hamid; I was afraid to in case it worsened his condition. Every time we spoke he was getting stronger—I could hear it in his voice. He kept asking me when my flight was, but each time I made some excuse until I felt he was well enough to take the news.

You're ... not coming?

No, I replied. I felt so bad. I tried to explain the one-way passport.

Don't worry about that, we can soon get you a new one. People are travelling here and leaving the country all the time.

But I did worry. I felt that I couldn't trust what he was saying. In the past he had said too many things to me and later gone back on his word. I tried to soften the blow:

Let me think about it some more.

He agreed, but as we said our goodbyes, I already knew my answer.

I felt so terrible about it. There he was, poor thing, with no close family to look after him at this awful time. He had good friends who were caring for him, though, but that isn't quite the same. I felt guilty about going back on what I'd said I'd do, but rationalised it by telling myself that I might not be able to get out again once there, especially if Hamid refused to give me his permission.

The beginning of the second year at university closely followed my decision not to go to Tehran, so, having made my decision to stay home, I contacted the course administrator to say that I'd be on the second year of the course programme starting that autumn (1997).

THE TIME WENT QUICKLY from October to Christmas. I was finding the coursework more difficult in the second year, so focused more on getting to grips with it, which took most of my attention.

Christmas came and went, as did the New Year, during which time I had regular contact with Hamid. I worried about how he was *really* coping and whether he was improving as much as he said he was when we talked over the phone. He had always been a great one for giving a good impression.

In February 1998 I received quite a lengthy letter from him which showed, on the one hand, that he was getting back on his feet and working again, and glad to be alive and making plans, but on the other, that his life-style had changed dramatically.

His letter began:

It really is a lovely day today, even by Iranian standards. The sky is absolutely clear and blue, and the mountains are so beautiful. As I travelled to work I could even see Mount Damavand very clearly in the distance. This must be the only capital city in the world with such beautiful mountain scenery.

One of these days I think I'll take the telecabin and go to the fifth station, just to be among the mountains and the snow. I should be all right, the altitude is only around 3,000 meters. The fresh air and scenery might do me a lot of good.

I felt so sad as I read this second paragraph, knowing that his joy was climbing and skiing in the mountains in Iran. Now, it seemed, he could only be an observer of the things he loved to do most. I was also sad because I wasn't there with him to empathise with his 'loss' and to help him.

I wanted to see him so much and found it difficult to concentrate on my work. Having come so close to death, nothing seemed more important than being with him. I thank God that I knew his friends would take good care of him.

THE SECOND ACADEMIC YEAR ENDED, and again, I just managed to scrape through it. My tutors had been very understanding about my situation and allowed me extra time to complete my assignments if I needed it.

I decided to move out of my sister's home during that summer and I found a room nearer the university. The move went smoothly and I was 'installed' in my new home for the beginning of the final year of the course. My house-mates were all students this time, and were aged nineteen to twenty-one, and a very lively, and, generally, nice bunch. I was surprised at how they were quite happy to sit and chat with me (being much older) over coffee, and how they made me feel part of the group. The house was only ever still - and quiet - when it was empty! When we were all in, it buzzed with activity and lots of music. A steady diet of comic-tragedy, depending mostly on how well their romantic relationships were functioning at the time, was a daily event, and one that often changed dramatically in the course of a week—or less!

The final year of the course began with me feeling quite nervous, knowing that this was the last and most important year to get through. I found the work quite hard, academically. Students were more focused this year and there was much competition between groups and quite a bit of frostiness from some who had been friendly in the previous two years. But despite all this, I managed to complete the course with a 2:2 and felt a sense of having achieved something I never would have done if I'd listened to those doubtful and discouraging voices, or if I was still living with my husband. I felt pleased with myself for daring to brave the unknown of higher education, and to graduate at the age of fifty-two. But I can see the advantage that younger people experience as they progress from school to university at the age of eighteen. For me, studying was quite difficult at this later age.

I found my time at university to be very positive and that because each stage of the course was targeted at achieving a higher level, I was always thinking ahead positively, instead of dwelling on all the disasters of the past, and this helped me realize that I could have a future that was good. Half of it was learning to make decisions for myself about my life and what I'd like to do with it—something I didn't have the right to do when I lived with Hamid.

I emerged from the course a different person in many ways. I thought differently, had much wider interests, and, more importantly, I was qualified for a better job. I felt more confident, more hopeful about the future, and that I was making good progress in life.

CHAPTER EIGHTEEN

GRADUATION

When graduation day arrived, the concert hall, where the ceremony was held, was filled with excited, new graduates and their guests. It was a great day for us all as, one by one, we went forward to receive our diplomas. It took time, obviously, to wade through the list but we didn't seem to mind and we were glad to see friends in such high spirits after being so worried during their exams.

At the end of the ceremony it took a while for everyone to file out of the hall. As we waited our turn to leave, I heard the faint strains of music and, listening more keenly, heard Vaughan William's, *Lark Ascending*, one of my favourite pieces of music, softly playing in the background. My heart leapt because I love this piece and in the moments that followed, I got an impression that this occasion was the stepping stone to things long awaited. I left the building filled with hope, wondering what God was going to do in my life from now on.

I still hadn't secured a job to go to following graduation, but was busy at that time typing up a manuscript on the works of

Graduation day

Hannah Moore, for Trent Editions, the English department's own imprint. One day, as I sat talking to the lecturer supervising this work, he looked straight at me and said that Personnel was about to advertise a new administrator's post for the English Department, and asked if I would be interested in it? I was surprised by his unexpected question, and replied that I'd like time to think about it. I took home a job description to help me make a decision.

Making this decision wasn't too difficult as I needed a job to pay my rent and pay off my student debts, and hey, if it didn't work out I could always find something else. But one advantage was that I'd be working among people I already knew and in familiar surroundings, so I decided to apply for it. After a somewhat chaotic interview (which still makes me laugh every time I think about it) I took on the part-time post as Research Administrator for English Research at Nottingham Trent University. I found work with a secretarial agency the rest of the time.

Within a short time I moved out of the shared house I'd been living in and found a very small, self-contained studio flat in West Bridgford, not too far from the campus and on a direct bus route. Pets were allowed there so the cat and I settled in to this little flat which became 'home' for the next eight years.

I had forgotten what privacy was. It felt so good to be able to close my front door; to not share a bathroom or kitchen; and having my own phone line with no-one listening in on my conversations was the icing on the cake! The location was very good because I could walk to most places, even to the city centre, or get a bus just over the road, if I needed to.

I contacted Hamid to give him my new address and the news about gaining a 2:2.

You'll be doing an MBA next, he said.

No, I don't think so, I replied as my mind raced ahead thinking of the work I needed to do the next day.

You could come to Iran and teach English here... His tone suggested he felt he could still persuade me to leave everything and go to him. Since he first left six years ago, he hadn't remotely suggested that he would come to England.

Just before Christmas that same year, I had a letter from Hamid together with a Christmas card. We were fast approaching the new Millennium, a time accompanied by so many forecasts, predictions, prophecies of what was going to happen to the world and its people. It was a bit of a scary time for me simply because I felt we were entering a new era that would be different from any I had known before. The great 'unknown' coupled with fear can be paralysing.

In his card Hamid wrote, jokingly: *I hope to see you more in this century than in the last one! Love, Hamid.*

MY FLAT WAS SITUATED ON the second floor of an old house on a quiet road, and quite a safe place to live. It must have been the top two bedrooms of the original house. The larger, en suite room with a tall, bay window alcove was my living room/bedroom, and the smaller room the kitchen. The kitchen was about two and a half metres square with a sloping ceiling and a window that looked out on to a fire escape. This was my escape route to safety—providing I could scramble through the small window on the back wall just above the sink!

The cat loved to snooze in the sun on the small, metal platform at the top of the steps there, while keeping a lazy eye on any passing bird. On wakening, she'd dozily lay on her back batting the odd fly or wasp buzzing round her, her black fur shining in the sun. Then, rolling on her side, and in no hurry to move, her eyes began spotting every flying thing.

With head dipped, and up on all fours now, she'd stretch out her front legs with all her might, and complete the waking experience with a big yawn. Sitting a minute or two wondering what to do next, she then began licking her chest and legs, and manicuring her claws by biting them for the next few minutes. After which, she'd silently meander down the steps and disappear into the neighbouring gardens.

As the weeks went by, I managed to wedge some large pots and troughs there and filled them with pretty, colourful flowers to look out on to as I washed the dishes. I never felt alone while the cat was with me; she was God's gift to help me through tough times.

THE PACE OF MY JOB WAS QUITE FAST and because it was a new

post, there was no-one to guide me through it except my boss, who was busy himself, most of the time. So I was left to find out most things myself, which turned out to be no bad thing because I learned not to depend on others when I could do the job myself.

Things were slightly less hectic and a bit more relaxed at the end of the academic year. The summer months were a time to reorganise and catch up on things that had been put on one side during the busy spells. I also liked to tag any left-over leave onto the end of the August Bank Holiday, just to give me a bit of a break before the new academic year began.

By the time October came, the university was in full swing. Academics, admin staff and maintenance men were rushing about trying to get everything ready to start the new academic year. Bewildered 'freshers' trying to find their way around the campus were the most frequent visitors to my office.

My birthday was later on in the month and Marj contacted me to see if I would like to go out for lunch on the day, which was a Sunday, and of course, I said I'd love to.

Quite a few months before this, I'd received a letter from Hamid pressing me to make a decision about going to live with him in Iran. He said:

Since your graduation I hope you've had time to think about what you want to do next. As you know, I would like you to come here so that we can live together.

We had been separated for seven years, by this time, and I

was just starting to make a little headway.

He continued:

When I look at other people's lives, it seems to me that, despite all the problems we've had, we still have a lot more in common than a lot of other couples I know, especially in the way we look at life. Besides, after all this time, the idea of each of us going our own separate ways and living the rest of our lives alone or with other people, seems absurd to me.

You may know me well enough by now, dear reader, to understand how I found it hard to answer this letter, so I put off doing so for quite a long time. I tried to weigh up what had happened between us during those seven years of separation, which showed nothing positive had happened during that entire time. I began listing the negatives:

1) Absolutely no support all this time.
2) Very irregular contact.
3) Made no attempt to come to see me in the UK during this time.
4) Didn't seem too concerned when I'd experienced bad episodes of ill health.
5) Would need my husband's permission to leave Iran.
6) Would be a foreigner there.
7) Am female.
8) Christian, not Muslim.
9) Would have no 'voice' there.

It wasn't looking good; I knew that if I went to Iran

this time I would be trapped. The answer was emphatically 'no', but I found it so hard to tell him. We had been together for twenty three years and separated for seven more, more than half my lifetime at that time.

About late September, I kept having a recurring thought about answering this letter, so much so, that it began to seem like the most important thing to do, so I sat down one night and re-read Hamid's letter in order to send a reply. I began writing, pointing out the reasons for not going to Iran from the list I'd made, and suggested that he could still come back to the UK and live here.

I then started writing about what I saw as our main problems, which were, having different religious faiths and different cultural values, and told him that they, in my opinion, would never be compatible, particularly under the new regime in Iran. Then at this point I had a very strong urge to tell him to come clean with God, to repent of any sin in his life and turn to Christ. I continued writing for seven pages giving reasons why he should do this, then suddenly finished the letter. By this time it was late in the night, and, feeling full of anxiety and distress, I left the letter on the table and went to bed.

I read it through over breakfast the next morning, but again, felt hesitant about sending it. I knew in my heart that this would be the severance of our relationship, so put off posting it for almost three weeks. But, by this time, something was prompting me with a sense of urgency to get the letter in the post, so I packed it in an envelope and took it to the post office. Normally a letter took five to seven days to reach its destination in Iran. I kept thinking about how Hamid might receive what I'd written, but still felt that I'd written what was in my heart and the right thing.

The following week at work went quite quickly, and I was glad, because I was looking forward to celebrating my birthday with my sister the coming Sunday. Weekends were usually taken up by doing chores on Saturdays and church on Sundays. So, when Saturday came, I was busy cleaning up my little flat, and as I stood cleaning the yellow sink, I suddenly thought to pray for Hamid as he should have received my letter by now. I threw up a prayer while still working on the sink:

Lord will you take Hamid into Your... I stopped. What was I saying? The next word was *presence*. Shocked by this I became fearful because it sounded as if he had died.

Refusing to accept that, I carried on cleaning the sink when, with eyes wide open, an image began to appear in my mind. A tall, slender, long-robed figure, whose head was not visible, scooped up a very small, yet adult Hamid in the palm of His hand, then placed him in the crook of His arm. Then the image left me. I was terrified because, again, I thought that Hamid had died. I tried to forget about it and carried on with my chores.

The next day - my birthday - my sister arrived to take me out to lunch and we spent the rest of the day together. The following day, Monday, I went off to work as usual and the same on Tuesday. I was busily caught up doing various tasks that morning when the office phone rang.

Hello, I said hurriedly.

Oh hello. Bobbi, is that you?

I recognised the voice of my dear friend Eileen who lived in Wales.

Thank goodness we've found you. I'm afraid we've got some sad news for you. I'll let you talk to David.

I was still in business mode.

What is it? I replied, mechanically.

I heard David's calm and soothing voice.

Hello, Bobbi. We're so sorry to have to tell you like this over the phone, but Sharon and her husband contacted us to tell us that Hamid has had a fatal heart attack. He died last Friday. Sharon and her husband were too upset to tell you and asked us to tell you, instead. If we had been nearer we would have come to you to be with you when we broke the news.

The words didn't sink in straight away.

Are you all right? He asked.

Yes, yes, I'm fine.

I didn't know what to say to my dear friend, this Godly man who had been used by God in such a powerful way to bring about change in my life - and many others - through his God-given healing ministry.

Is anyone with you in the office?

Not at the moment, but I'm OK. I just need a minute or two to take it in.

He talked to me until he was sure I was able to deal with it. We said goodbye, and I slumped into the chair in front of my desk. Suddenly I started panicking.

I must go and tell someone.

My emotions were racing now and I was breathing rapidly, I burst out of the office and headed for a Christian friend's office. He was talking with someone when I got there so I waited outside, trying to keep the tears at bay. He saw me through the window and came out of his office.

Hello Bobbi. Do you think you could come back later, I'm in the middle of a meeting at the moment?

I couldn't wait.

I've just had a phone call to say that my husband has had a fatal heart attack in Iran.

And with that came the tears. He postponed his meeting then quickly arranged for me to see the chaplain, who then contacted Marj to come and take me home.

EVERYTHING SEMED TO COME TO A HALT over the next couple of days, I can't even recall where I was during that time. But I do remember being at home on the third day after I'd heard the news about Hamid, and that my sister was with me. By then I felt I wanted to be on my own for a while so that I could be myself and feel what I could only truly feel when alone with my thoughts. So I asked Marj if she'd leave me to mull things over. She understood and agreed to leave on the condition that I'd contact her if I needed her.

After she left, I sat in the mid-green chair at my desk near the bay window weeping for a long time. Then a startling thought jolted me back into the present:

IT WAS FINISHED: MY MARRIAGE HAD COME TO AN END.

The decision had been made for us by someone other than ourselves, and the thing I'd feared for most of my married life–Hamid's death (untimely at fifty-six) had happened.

Angry questions began dominating my emotions: Why had our life together been like it had—unhappy and traumatic—when there had been so much in our favour? Why had he opposed so much of the person I was by trying to squash me? Why hadn't he loved me the way I wanted him to? And why had his death happened *now*, with so many unresolved issues between us, leaving no solutions and no answers to these questions? Other startling thoughts gathered momentum: *we would never again* meet up or talk over the phone: *there was now no hope* of sorting things out, and *no* possible future *reconciliation*.

I T W A S F I N I S H E D!

My thoughts, like a taught rope when severed, were reeling round and round in my head. I floundered, fearing the future unknown with its hopes dashed. My thoughts and secret hopes had been geared towards reconciliation in the depths of my heart, and Death exposed that, making me face up to the truth that I still loved Hamid, despite everything that had gone before.

I wanted to yell and scream, to hit out at someone, at something. The unleashed power of this emotional turmoil was frightening; yet even more frightening was that I became aware of my thoughts racing out of control: I had to get a grip on things or else I'd 'go under'. I forced myself to remain seated whilst trying to take control of my emotions. My chest was so sore and head racked with such pain, I didn't know which way to turn to find relief.

I looked out at the sky-line searching for answers above the high-rise buildings in the distance. I felt no connection now with this city I was born and bred in and where I'd spent most of my life.

Tears splashed softly on the desk in front of me as my confused thoughts began slipping into a formless, charcoal-grey uncertainty with no signposts along the way. The baffled blankness of not knowing what to do or expect now brought everything to a standstill.

Then, at that point, and quite out of the blue, the picture I'd had a few days before of Hamid being picked up and placed in the crook of the figure's arm, popped into my mind. I remembered the prayer: *Lord, please take Hamid into Your...presence.* A sudden rush of recognition hit me at full force: ***God had saved Hamid*** and he was now safe with Him for eternity! My sore heart leapt and I began praising God and singing, laughing and crying all at the same time.

Exquisite, unspeakable joy knowing that Father had heard and answered my prayer! I remembered also that many others all over the world had prayed for Hamid and for his salvation for many years: my prayers were over a period of twenty-nine years. God heard us all and answered.

As I was writing this thirteen years later, it occurred to me that we ***WILL*** see each other again—in Heaven—because I, too, belong to God. We will spend *eternity together*, with God, with Jesus and The Holy Spirit - The Trinity, and with all those faithful believers through the ages, patriarchs and prophets - and that *we will be changed.* (1 Corinthians 15: 52.) What a stunning thought!

As I write, the date is February 14th, 2014: I'd forgotten it was Valentine's Day.

CHAPTER NINETEEN

HOPES RAISED

It wasn't long after this that I returned to work. People were kind and sympathetic but I couldn't contain my joy at what God had shown me and I kept telling everyone about it! To me it was so wonderful, but to my listeners, well...who knows what they thought!

There were times, though, as the weeks went by, when I felt sad and regretted the way life had been, but I think that's how it is when you lose someone, especially after experiencing difficulties in your relationship with them.

THE PHONE WAS RINGING rather more than usual as people were hearing the news about Hamid. Jallil, a close friend of ours who lived in Iran, phoned me regularly at this time to make sure I was OK. Then one day when answering a call, a voice said:

Is that you Bobbi?

Yes, I replied.

How are you Bobbi Jan? This is Shirin speaking: do you remember me?

She hadn't been in touch for years.

Yes I do, I replied.

Bobbi Jan, are you coming to Iran? We need you here with your marriage certificate and ID card so that we can sort out the inheritance.

Inheritance?? I hadn't even thought about any legacy!

I won't be coming to Iran, I said matter-of-factly, knowing that in this situation I wouldn't be at all safe.

Oh...she paused, *you do know that Hamid has died, don't you?*

Yes, I replied, knowing full well what was uppermost in her mind.

If you are not coming can you send us the documents so that we can action the process?

Her family stood to inherit a good chunk of Hamid's assets. My share should have been one eighth of the total, according to Islamic law. (Good job I wasn't living there when he died, I would have had to sell my home—leaving me homeless—and the money would have been divided between us).

I'll have to get a lawyer to act on my behalf, I'll let you know his name and address when I've found someone.

If you need help with anything let us know, she urged.

Her parting sentence made me smile. She was the daughter of the person who'd tried to gain legal possession of our apartment, if you remember, when Hamid first arrived back in Iran. I decided she wasn't to be trusted at all.

The thought of receiving an inheritance was music to my

ears. Only a few weeks before I'd been so broke, I hadn't been able to afford to buy the week's groceries, and my sister had had to give me money so that I could eat!

I'd struggled financially for a very long time; years, in fact. Every month my salary would go into the bank and by the end of the following third week, my account was overdrawn—not because I was reckless with my money—but because I wasn't earning enough to cover my outgoings. I struggled with poor health which meant that I had to ask my boss if I could reduce my hours of work to four days a week, just so that I could continue working, and to which he agreed. But, of course, that reduced my salary. I seemed to be in a no-win situation.

SHIRIN'S PHONECALL WAS ONLY THE BEGINNING of a long, drawn out, legal saga lasting almost five years.

I contacted a trusted Iranian friend to ask his advice. He said he'd heard from a friend of a good lawyer in Tehran who could help.

Go to your solicitor and get a Power of Attorney document for this lawyer to act on your behalf in Tehran, he said.

This I did and posted it with all the other documents needed to my friend, who then took them to Tehran with him on his next visit.

He met the lawyer and gave him the background relating to my situation and the reason I wouldn't be travelling to Iran, then, confidently, left everything in the lawyer's hands, trusting him to act on my behalf. Well, what a mistake 'trusting him' turned out to be! But we didn't know that at the time.

My friend kept in touch with the lawyer, every so often, to find out how things were progressing, and he kept assuring him that he was working on the case but that others involved weren't co-operating. I had asked specifically for Hamid's death certificate, which I needed to legally prove that my marital status had changed. Did he send it? No, he didn't. Even after repeated requests he failed to come up with the goods.

My first reaction was angry disbelief. How could they (the others involved) be so heartless at a time like this? I was really upset by their despicable attitude. But they maintained their resistance for the next five years and refused to co-operate in any way; so you can imagine what a blow it was when the lawyer told my friend:

She's a Christian, anyway, and doesn't stand a chance of gaining anything!

If that was the case, why didn't he say that in the first place? Why did he let it drag on for five, long years?

I was very upset at this because, again, I was being discriminated against because of my faith in God. I gave up pursuing the case at this point. The lawyer had showed me that there was no justice there for women, or for people of real faith in the Living God. The whole thing proved to be fruitless and a complete waste of time. But it did reveal the true nature and character of those involved and I wondered what might have happened to me if I'd gone to Iran, as was suggested...

I felt huge resentment at this as it seemed like another smack in the face, compounding everything else connected with Hamid leaving me. I became thoroughly unhappy by thoughts that nothing at all good had come out of my relationship with him.

But this in itself was a learning curve for me because I later learnt that, if you hold on to your resentments, your personality starts to change. You start to mistrust and dislike people more, you decide to withdraw those good qualities of love, kindness and generosity to others, and as you harbour your grudges, your joy disappears. In turn, these things cause others to be more cautious in relating to you, and some move away altogether. Eventually, you start getting sick with all sorts of illnesses and with a good dose of self-pity. I started getting bad colds and sometimes the flu and I would always be 'catching up' at work because I regularly went down with something or other and had to have time off. There was never any time to convalesce or any money to take a holiday to help me recover.

It took a few years for me to realize *why* I was trapped in this vicious circle. And it took a few more years to realize that the ball to healing was actually in my court. The name of this particular ball was called *forgiveness.*

I felt justified in hanging on to my resentments, and I begrudged having to forgive my offenders for a long time. But, you know, it only made things worse. Every time I was treated unfairly, I added that to the list, until an enormous pile of resentments had built up. I also felt pretty miserable with it! It took me a while to realize that life 'ain't fair' a lot of the time, and that the sooner I wised up to that and forgave an offence, the sooner I'd be free to receive God's forgiveness and healing, and could then move out from all the bad stuff that held me back.

In The Lord's Prayer, we ask God to: *Forgive us our sins as we forgive those who sin against us,* and to *deliver us from evil.* So, when we forgive, God also forgives us and with that comes a change in our attitudes; a deeper love and gratitude towards God because we see the change that's taken place; healing in whatever area God's knows we need healing i.e. body, mind, spirit; and a different perspective on things. Jesus also said in Matthew 6: v.14-15: *If you forgive men when they sin against you, your Heavenly Father will also forgive you. But if you do not forgive men their sins, your Father will not forgive your sins.*

When it finally dawned on me that my sins wouldn't be forgiven by God unless *I forgave* those who'd sinned against me, I very quickly began trying to put forgiveness in to practise. I came up against obstacle after obstacle as I tried, because I was angry, and felt I had every right to be angry, about life's bitter blows. But, you know, in hindsight, I now realize that God was challenging me with the power of the Cross, and what Jesus accomplished there.

This was a deeper level in my journey of faith and one that would strip away any attitudes that didn't put God first in my life. Anger, resentment, bitterness, all come first when we want to hang on to them. God stands by, waiting...waiting for us to put things right with Him and to make Him first in everything; waiting to heal us, waiting to make us 'new' in those places that have held us captive for years. It's all for our benefit.

Some thirteen years on, I still struggle, sometimes, to do the right thing when I experience personal injustice. But I now know that forgiveness is God's greatest action of transforming that which is unholy into that which is holy. When we forgive, we can then genuinely pray for those who have offended us, thus bringing them before God with genuine concern about their salvation, instead of harbouring ill-will towards them. Life here is a hundred years max., but eternity is forever. Because I know God and know that He loves me, I want to be with Him for eternity, but I know I won't make it unless I am forgiven by God, and have forgiven those who have sinned against me. The process is ongoing.

BACK AT WORK AFTER HAMID'S DEATH proved to be both therapeutic as well as busy. It helped me concentrate on what was happening in the present rather than what had gone before. I enjoyed my job and it turned out to be the most interesting job I'd had, so far. So time went by quickly. I also learned a lot.

One day, as I was chatting to a colleague, she mentioned that she had an allotment near to where I lived. My immediate response was:

Oh, I'd love an allotment!

Well, why don't you go down and see if you can get one, they're only

£15 a year?

I'd longed for a garden to grow fruits and vegetables in, a place to potter on a nice day, away from my second-storey studio flat, with no access to the garden at the back of the building, and a view of black tarmac at the front.

So, off I went the following Saturday to find Pete, the chap in charge of renting out the allotments. To my amazement, there were about ten gardens up for grabs! I decided on a double corner plot (just shows how inexperienced I was) but I liked the high hedges for privacy (never thinking about the work they'd need to keep them trimmed). It had an enormous Victoria Plum tree, the boughs of which were thickly laden with young, green plums. I was thrilled to bits at the thought of harvesting copious amounts of ripe, delicious plums. They, alone, reimbursed me the amount I paid for the annual rent! There were also three apple trees; a large blackcurrant bush; countless blackberries and elderberries; and a battered shed at the back-end of the garden with a big hole in the roof that let the rain in. I took to it immediately and was thrilled to have this wild, overgrown patch to spend my spare time in, and at the thought of growing my own food.

There's nothing to compare with being down there through the different seasons and in all types of weather. The joy of suddenly spotting a little red-breasted robin hopping close by, keeping me company as I dug the ground. The heavy dew in the quiet, early morning glistening on a huge spider's web, sparkling in the sun. The openness of the vast, beautiful, blue sky on a sunny day. Planting and waiting for those first tiny leaves to poke through the soil. Nurturing and then reaping the harvest of all the work put in. It was back to nature and a place where time didn't matter - except when sowing and reaping, of course. It not only fed my body, but also nourished my soul. I was constantly amazed at how beautiful and clever nature is, and at how easy it is to grow delicious fruit and vegetables.

Unbeknown to me at the time, the minister of my church and two other friends shared an allotment opposite mine. When I found out, it was good to know they were nearby when I was working down there alone.

I ENJOYED THE FELLOWSHIP AT MY NEW CHURCH. I had met and made friends with lots of people and benefited greatly from our minister's teaching. His knowledge and love of God was (and I'm sure, still is) very deep, and I developed a great respect for him because of this. His faith encouraged my faith and my personal walk with God.

Sometime during 2006 I was in church listening to someone speaking about prayer, about the importance of prayer and how to listen to God as we pray. At the end of her talk she asked if anyone thought that God had spoken to them at some point, and asked them to share it with her after the service. I sat there thinking for a while and decided to see what she thought about a recurring word I'd had over the last few months that kept popping into my mind during my prayer times at home. So after the service was over I said:

I'm not sure whether this is from God or my own thoughts, so I'm giving this word to you to test.

What's the word? she asked.

Recession. I replied.

I left it with her to pray about and asked her to let me have any feedback. I waited a few weeks but didn't hear from her, so decided to ask her if she'd had any confirmation about the word.

No, she said, *I haven't.*

So I accepted that and didn't pursue it any more.

Then in less than two years I remembered it again when the biggest global, economic collapse I've seen began happening, and I realized that God had given a warning over a long period about what was going to happen.

I wasn't sure about the word at the time, so didn't share it with anyone until that day at church, partly because I didn't think it would be accepted as a word from God.

But what it showed me was that, over this, we weren't spiritually sharp enough to take it on board, and that needs to be looked at. *God is still speaking to us*, trying to get through to us. Are we still listening, and do we want to hear what He has to say?

CHAPTER TWENTY

GOODBYE, MY FRIEND

My poor cat had been diagnosed with diabetes about fifteen months before she began showing signs of distress because of it. Her health deteriorated hugely over the following year by which time I was injecting her twice a day with insulin. She became so ill at times that I had to face the fact that, sooner or later, I would have to make the decision to have my dear, furry companion, Zoe, faithful through thick and thin, put down. It was such an emotional time. She'd moved house with me so many times, I'm really surprised she didn't just wander off, as some cats do. I couldn't bear the thought of making the decision to end her life—I felt I didn't have the right to do so. Dave, my dear brother-in-law, gave me some very wise advice:

The vet will know when the time comes, let him make the decision, he said.

His words took away the heavy responsibility of making that decision, but every time I took Zoe to see the vet after that, I wondered if I'd return home without her. Surprisingly, she lasted a few months longer, until one day, I came home from work to find she'd collapsed on the living-room floor and was barely breathing. Anyone who's had a pet they loved can imagine how I felt. Panicking, I scraped her up off the floor and put her in her pet carrier, trying not to hurt her. She always hated being confined in the carrier and fought me every time I tried to get her into it, but there was no resistance this time. I raced down the stairs and out to the car, keys in one hand, cat in the other, and fell into the car. All I could think about was getting her to the vet, hoping that she would perform some miracle to save her. I turned the ignition key—no response. I grabbed the carrier and raced back upstairs to phone a taxi.

It'll be there in twenty minutes, said the bland voice at the other end.

But I need a taxi NOW—my cat's dying!

Sorry dear, came the reply, *that's the soonest we can get someone to you.*

In floods of tears by this time and unable to think clearly, I ran down to my neighbour on the next floor, who, thankfully, was at home.

Don't worry, I'll take you, he said, promptly springing into action, and I followed as he took Zoe down to his car.

I sat in the vet's waiting room clutching Zoe, trying not to cry. I think the other person waiting there understood something was seriously wrong and didn't try to engage me in conversation. Rob had nipped back home by this time, leaving his phone number with me. When our turn came, the vet said:

She's in bad shape. I can give her an injection now to end her suffering, or we can keep her alive for the next twenty-four hours to see how she responds to treatment, but you will have to take her to our hospital on Clumber Road.

I chose the latter, and phoned Rob who came and drove us to the hospital where I left Zoe in the hands of another vet. It was a very sad night without her, knowing that she was so poorly.

Around eleven o'clock the next morning the office phone rang. It was the vet saying that Zoe had made a remarkable recovery. I was thrilled. He then added:

But she's behaving like a wild animal. I suggest that you have her put down straight away.

Can you delay it till I can be there with her? I pleaded.

He agreed, reluctantly, and said goodbye. Again, in floods of tears, my thoughts desperate and irrational, were coupled with the fear of someone coming in the office and finding me in this upset state. On reflection, it was interesting to see how I tried remaining in 'work mode' while breaking down completely. A young colleague came through the door.

What's happened? He was upset to see me crying.

The vet's just phoned to say that the cat's got to be put down.

He, poor thing, didn't know what to say; he'd never seen me in this state before.

I don't know what to do, he said helplessly.

He left the office, and I phoned Marj.

Dave will come and pick you up now to take you to the vet's, she said.

I went and told my boss what was happening. He was sympathetic and told me to go and 'do what I had to do'.

SHALL I COME IN WITH YOU? asked Dave as he parked outside the hospital.

No, I replied, *I want to be alone with her.*

You're sure you'll be all right?

Yes.

I climbed the steps to the old, newly-painted green door, rang the bell and waited. A voice from the intercom asked if I had an appointment, I replied, I had. The door opened electronically, and, knowing what lay ahead, I stepped over the threshold feeling upset and anxious. I told the receptionist who I was and she asked me to wait in the waiting room. I waited quite a long time before the vet, clad in a green 'theatre' gown, called my name.

She took me through to a side room where a long, grey table jutted out near the wall to the left. She left the room and in seconds, re-appeared with Zoe in a carrier. She let her out on top of the table, while at the same time, telling me that Zoe had been behaving like a wild animal and that they couldn't get anywhere near her.

Even getting her into the carrier just now was difficult, she said.

(I should have mentioned that at the beginning when I first

took her there!)

I was astonished to see how thin she was. When she was at home I hadn't noticed so much, but now, after not seeing her for twenty four hours, she looked really skinny.

The vet tried to attach a tube to her paw. She shrieked and began hissing while backing-off into a corner of the table.

She been like this since she arrived, the vet said.

She was so distressed she began vomiting. My poor puss, what a sorry state she was in. I reached for her, wanting to take her in my arms for the last time but when I picked her up, she stank of urine.

She was still shrieking and growling as I held her under her chest, her back legs still on the table. I kept talking to her hoping she'd recognise my voice. I gently rocked her in my hand, speaking familiar words to her and stroking her head. It took a long time to quieten her, but eventually, she stopped crying and became calm. I continued speaking to her, and, without thinking, my head just turned and looked at the long tube attached to her paw.

Shall I do it now? The vet didn't waste a second.

Yes, I replied.

She injected a mega dose of anaesthetic into the tube and, within seconds, Zoe lay limp in my hand.

Efficiently, the vet took her from me and laid her on her side, removing all tubes, clips, etc., as quickly as she could.

Oh look at her eyes, I said, *they look beautiful.*

The vet quickly closed them with her index finger. She

then disappeared through a door and came back with a pink towel.

Pink for a girl, I said, as she carefully wrapped her in it.

She then put Zoe into her carrier for the last time. This time there was no refusing to go in, no having to chase her round the room, and no bleeding, claw-marks on my arms and shoulders. The struggle had ended - and so had her suffering.

The vet placed the carrier on a chair and asked me to wait in the reception area. She appeared a few minutes later with the lifeless, pink-towelled bundle and a sympathetic smile as she handed the carrier to me.

I walked over to the desk to pay the bill.

That's £168, please, the receptionist said.

I automatically wrote the cheque and handed it over to her, then turned and walked out of the building and down the steps to the car. I was so grateful to see Dave waiting for me when I came out of there.

Are you OK? he asked.

Yes, I replied, *I'm OK.*

It was one of those situations where I had no other option to do anything else. It was a case of having to face it and go through with it.

We took her to my favourite place to bury her. Dave had a spade in the car ready to dig a deep hole. As he was digging, I took Zoe out of the carrier, speaking to her for the last time. Her limp body was still warm and I hugged her for the last time before Dave gently lowered her down into her little grave. The pet I loved was there under my favourite tree, and later on, whenever I was there, I felt really close to her.

That night, alone in my tiny flat without her, was both sad and strange. Except for the night she'd spent at the vet's, she had always been there with me, getting under my feet, or sleeping next to me.

Because of her illness she'd been my total focus for the last two years. My whole timetable was planned around Zoe: her injections, her feeding times, making her comfortable and safe so she didn't fall downstairs in her weaker moments. She was eighteen when she died—a good age for a cat, I'm told. I did everything I could to help her.

I wasn't used to living without her padding around the flat, or quietly watching me as I worked. Several times afterwards, I thought I saw her shadow walking through the doorway into the next room, or just behind me for a second as I moved away from the kitchen sink. But then, I knew her pattern of behaviour like the back of my hand. My mind was still programmed to her daily activities, so I think, in absent-minded moments, I expected her to be there doing the things she always did. These experiences weren't spooky at all, because I realized my imagination was playing along with the routine we'd had for such a long time.

Again, people were so kind to me, especially those with pets, because they understood how dear Zoe had become to me.

CHAPTER TWENTY ONE

ON TO NEW THINGS

During 2005, the university underwent a massive re-structuring programme. Jobs and staff were being scrutinised, and this was followed by a general 'sifting' across the board. Some people lost their jobs, some were demoted, some were promoted, and others, like myself, were re-grouped and integrated into existing teams of administrators working together in a large office.

Until this time, I'd worked for, and under the supervision of academics working on research projects. I had my own office, a lot of autonomy, and I loved the work I did—which held my interest in the job. I learned a lot from doing this type of work, which also helped develop my own personal interests.

When I was re-grouped all that changed. I came under the authority of an admin. office manager and a big shift in mind-set regarding my work. I didn't like being in the new office—and there were some who didn't like me being there!

As time went on, the situation became almost intolerable for me, until one day, I lost my temper over something and was punished for it. I was very angry at the unfair way I'd been treated, and stewed on it until I felt that the only option I had was to leave. It was January 2007 and I was eligible for retirement at the end of the year, so I decided to take it. I was more than ready to move out of there and on to the next stage of my life.

It has since proved to be the right decision, and has offered me a new freedom to explore and develop areas of interest I've had for many years.

AS I LOOK FORWARD NOW, the future lies open before me and only God knows what He has planned for me. But I'll trust Him with that, because, as I look back over my life, so far, I can see how His mighty hand has brought me safely to where I am today. It's very clear to me that He knew what lay ahead of me in life, and that I was going to need Him. I know for sure, that without His guidance and protection, I wouldn't have made it through the difficulties.

So in gratitude to Him who has done great things for me personally, I want to end by saying:

To God be the glory.

Printed in Great Britain
by Amazon